OUT ON A LIMB
A Journal of Wisconsin Birding

OUT ON A LIMB

A Journal of
Wisconsin Birding

by
Roy Lukes

With illustrations by
Charlotte Lukes

Roy Lukes
Charlotte Lukes

Aug. 22, 1979

PINE STREET PRESS
Baileys Harbor, Wisconsin
1979

CONTENTS

ILLUSTRATIONS

INTRODUCTION

A very feisty kildeer nested in my folks' pea patch one summer when I was about six or seven years old. A huge sand pile, where my brothers and I spent long hours playing, was situated next to the north side of the garage and was much closer to the nervous bird's nest than she appreciated. Not only is that the first bird eposide in my life that I can clearly recall, but I do believe the excitement of watching that killdeer inspired me to become a birder.

Several years later, when I was a fifth grader at the Kewaunee Public School, a pair of robins built their nest in the cedar hedge right next to the top of a pair of steps leading down to the playground. Fortunately the nest was placed slightly below eye level and within a foot from the outside of the bushes, making it possible for me to follow the activities of this pair. Undoubtedly this suspenseful drama, carefully peeked into several times each school day until the young fledged and left the nest, greatly reinforced and strengthened my fondness for birds and nature in general.

Dr. Hugh Talbot, biology professor at the University of Wisconsin-Oshkosh, motivated me to the challenging and disciplined lure of the list. How I worked to be the first in the spring to report a scarlet tanager, brown thrasher, or rufous-sided towhee. More than once I was caught ''out on a limb'' spending too much time birding on the way to school and had to run the last mile or so to be on time for my first class.

Birding literally saved the day for me during my two-year hitch in the U.S. Army. Many hours spent observing scissor-tailed flycatchers, red-bellied woodpeckers, western kingbirds, and others helped ease the pain of homesickness and boredom. In fact the scissor-tailed flycatcher, to this day, continues to be one of my favorite birds—even though I haven't seen once since 1955!

One of the first things I did during my initial year of teaching at Shorewood Hills in Madison was to introduce my combination 7th and 8th grade class to birding. My most successful approach involved taking groups of six or seven students into the field early in the morning to study birds until it was time for school to begin. Having only boys or only girls in each group proved to be a decided advantage. In fact, each of the four or five groups had great fun challenging one another for the longest list.

I was tearfully surprised that first Christmas when I opened a gift from the students and found the two-record set of bird songs published by Cornell University! I used them repeatedly with that class and with many more groups in later years. The records are still in good condition and being used 23 years later.

A particular song on one of the records, which both fascinated and amused that first class (and me!), was that of the yellow-headed blackbird. Imagine my disbelief one Saturday morning during the spring of 1956, at Picnic Point along the south shore of Lake Mendota in Madison, upon hearing, of all things, a yellow-headed blackbird. Dr. Robert McCabe, of the University of Wisconsin Wildlife Management Department, told me later that this was one of several pair that were transplanted there as part of an experimental project.

The following Monday morning I informed my bird-watcher students that I planned to go out to Picnic Point the next morning at sunrise. I had no trouble getting a group of about six, including Neil Reudisili, to accompany me, even though I said nothing about the possibility of hearing and seeing the yellow-headed blackbird. We had hiked around nearly the entire perimeter of the little marsh where I had hoped for the surprise, but no luck. Suddenly, just as I began to think we were not going to hear it, there came that unbelievable rusty gate-hinge sound, which on this morning was real music to my ears. Neil Reudisili looked at me—how lower jaw dropping slightly and his eyes nearly popping out—and said over and over, "HOLY COW! A YELLOW-HEADED BLACKBIRD! HOLY COW! A YELLOW-HEADED BLACKBIRD!"

Never before that beautiful morning, nor since during the following 21 years of teaching, has one of my birding groups been as thrilled with "the find" as those 7th graders were hearing and seeing their first yellow-headed blackbird. Neil Reudisili is now a Lutheran minister, and I hope he responds as wonderfully and with similar enthusiasm to his parishioners as he did to his first yellow-headed blackbird! I have an idea that he does.

To me, this is what birding is all about—the pleasure, challenge, learning, and discipline related to the study, but perhaps more important, the great fellowship it invariably tends to create. No one, in all my years of bird study, has exemplified this more strongly than Samuel Robbins, who many of us birders think is Wisconsin's leading ornithologist.

I give special thanks to Reverend "Sam" Robbins who inspired me more than he could imagine while he was leading a field trip during the annual convention of the Wisconsin Society for Ornithology (W.S.O.) at Adams-Friendship in the late 1950s. This was the first W.S.O. convention I attended.

Edward Peartree, of Oconomowoc, housed and fed me on many weekends during the early 1960s, while he was teaching me the techniques and skills of bird banding and the use of Japanese mist nets in capturing birds. I am also very grateful to Ed for his many hours of teaching me about birds in the field during my first years of birding.

For much of my best learning about birds in the field, I must also thank other good friends such as Carl and Dorothy Frister, Harold Wilson, Murl Deusing, Dr. Charles Kemper, Drs. Frederich and Francis Hamerstrom. Drs. Frederich and Marguerite Baumgartner, and Tom Erdman. I respect their great knowledge and appreciate their guidance and help.

I am deeply indebted to the *Door County Advocate*, the *Appleton Post Crescent*, and the *Green Bay Press Gazette* for having first published the essays contained in this book and for giving me their earnest support in our putting some of them into seasonal story form in *Out On A Limb*.

Lastly, I give my heartfelt thanks to my wife, Charlotte, for the many hours of help she has provided with birding groups, annual Christmas bird counts, breeding bird surveys, spring woodcock counts, as well as her sharp eyes and her companionship while birding from day to day. The completion of this book was possible only because of her many hours of proofreading and correcting the text, as well as creating the drawings.

Shrike Alert!

The first thing I heard when the radio-alarm went off at six this morning was the weather report. Even the announcer's teeth chattered when he said the wind-chill factor was between 40 and 50 degrees below zero F.! The deep layer of quilts felt warm, but unfortunately my wife's foot was gently nudging me out of bed even as I pulled the covers up around my chin.

I eased the kitchen window shade aside and shined a flashlight on the outdoor thermometer. That made me want more than ever to go back to bed. Ten below zero! One could easily imagine the biting arctic wind with long gnashing teeth threatening us to remain indoors.

The point I continually ponder this morning, as the gale-like wind makes shrill whistling noises in the chimney, pertains to the birds. Even though I've already chugged down a mug of coffee and the indoor temperature is up to 60, I still feel dreadfully cold. But consider a pine siskin, whose weight is less than one-half of an ounce. He is surviving outdoors at this second, where the temperature, based on the wind-chill factor, is 100 degrees colder! The very thought suddenly makes me feel much warmer.

Most of my Sunday morning was spent shoveling the long driveway. The snow wasn't especially deep, but rather wet and very heavy. It had rained steadily the day before producing two sizable puddles. Now they were surrounded with snow that looked disgustingly out of place. The temperature was dropping sharply and I was intent on getting the icy snow off the drive before it froze solid.

As I worked on the walk, I noticed a huge flock of evening grosbeaks who were especially noisy and very skittish. They fed for a moment or two, then wheeled in lively, boisterous unison high over the maple trees, finally landing in the tallest birch tree north of the garage. A smaller flock of about 30 to 40 siskins behaved in a similar manner, extremely nervous, as they fed and flew away, fed and flew away.

1

Finally, I pushed my shovel into a snowbank for a rest and sauntered over to the platform feeders for a closer look. When I got there the siskins were back at their favorite occupation, eating the hulled sunflower seeds they were so adept at finding among the thousands of empty husks. Past experience had taught me to move ever so slowly toward them. Perhaps I could even touch one of them. Three feet, two feet, one foot. Now my face was about 10 inches from one of the fidgety little squirts.

Charlotte came out with the camera to photograph our private little conversation. The siskins lisped and chattered in a dainty plaintive way, and I, in turn, made high soft whistling sounds through my teeth. The whistlings may have been perfectly meaningless to the siskins, but they weren't to me. Suddenly, with explosive force, the tiny birds all took off and landed in the highest branches of the aspen tree overhead.

I said to Charlotte, "Don't these birds appear to be on edge?"

Before she could reply, she noticed a movement in the speckled alders. "NORTHERN SHRIKE!" she called out. No sooner had she given warning than the shrike made a flying pass at one of the nimble siskins and missed. The sleek gray and black "butcher bird" continued to soar upward and produced one of the most beautiful aerial maneuvers I have ever seen. Imagine a stunt plane doing a sweeping "loop-the-loop" while flying straight upward. That's exactly what the shrike did. The wind appeared to carry him along and—fortunately, for the siskins—the predator from the north headed south and away.

Within minutes the tiny birds were back at their second most important task of the day, eating. Their most important job by far was to remain constantly on guard for the shrike, to stay out of its clutches.

Now the little "half pints" carried on as they had so frequently in the past. Within a few minutes they were perched on my gloved hand, on my shoulder, or on top of my cap searching for the few hulled sunflower seeds placed there. Feisty, pesky, aggressive, and unwelcome are just a few of the adjectives some of our friends use in describing these tiny winter visitors. We, however, welcome them. They make us appreciate our supply of wood in the woodshed, the cozy old wood range in the kitchen, and even the ability to shovel the long driveway after each snowstorm. We gaze in awe at a pine siskin, weighing a scant forty-seven hundredths of one ounce and yet capable of surviving the stinging blasts of a 50-degree-below-zero January wind. And, indeed, we feel humble!

Nuthatch Cousins

Someone once asked me, "How much do you really benefit by watching birds?" I wonder whether he was implying that I spent too much time looking at those feathered creatures or whether he was questioning the worth of what Charlotte and I annually spend feeding them.

Even though it would be preposterous to attempt to place a dollars-and-cents figure on the benefits derived from bird-watching, I nevertheless thought that I could at least determine how much purchased food each bird was consuming in our backyard.

I estimated that during the first three weeks of December, approximately 125 different birds were attracted to our feeders daily: 30 black-capped chickadees, 75 evening grosbeaks, 7 woodpeckers, 8 nuthatches, 2 cardinals, and 3 blue jays. They consumed an average of six pounds of sunflower seeds a day, amounting to $1.08 per day. Each bird, by these figures, was consuming between eight-tenths and nine-tenths of one cent worth of seeds. I would say that it's certainly worth the price to obtain a half dozen views of a flashy male cardinal each day for less than a penny a day!

Two species whose day-to-day appearances have been extremely constant are the white-breasted and red-breasted nuthatches. But it is obvious, when visitors comment about the birds at our feeders, that these two species play "second fiddle" to the active and gaudy evening grosbeaks. Neither of the nuthatches is outwardly flashy nor attracts a great deal of attention. They are businesslike, scooting in for one seed then heading for the thicket to consume it.

The red-breasted nuthatch, smaller of the two, impresses me as being cheerful, high-spirited, sprightly, and dexterous. His white-breasted cousin appears to be straitlaced and unemotional by comparison. In fact, his gray, white, and black plumage resembles a business suit.

Perhaps "rust-breasted" nuthatch would be a better name than red-breasted, for some of them—most often females, but some males as well—exhibit pale buff feathers on their undersides, a far cry from red. A significant mark of identification is their long white eyebrow line that tends to highlight the black cap of the male and the dark blue-gray cap of the female.

Beginning bird-watchers frequently confuse nuthatches with the unrelated woodpeckers. Woodpeckers need their tails for support, in most instances, and cannot maintain their balance head downward on a tree as can the nuthatches. Both species of nuthatches have big feet, short tails, and are very likely to be seen with their heads pointed downward, necks extended outward at right angles to the tree. One foot is usually braced at a right angle to the other or even slightly backward.

Our November and December observations indicate there are more red-breasted nuthatches here now than in previous years. Even though they are thought of as permanent residents they are known to leave their most northerly ranges when the natural food supply diminishes.

An easy observation of the nuthatches and other birds coming to your winter feeders may enable you to be more helpful to them. Record the time of their last appearance before dark and their first appearance in the morning, and then calculate the length of their night, a period when they are obviously without food. You will most likely come up with at least 14 hours during December and early January. Available food in the late afternoon, especially when the birds have become dependent upon your handout, may be critical, so make a practice of setting out a few extra handfuls of seed each day at about 4 P.M. or earlier.

There are at least two other lifesaving aids you can easily construct for the birds. One is a brush pile. Place the heaviest branches on the inside, followed by thinner twigs; and, finally, cap it with a layer of evergreen boughs. The latter will help keep the inside of the shelter dry.

A roost box, shelter box, or whatever you wish to call it can be constructed from a wooden container about the size of an apple box, 12 by 14 by 18 inches. A single entrance is cut at the bottom of one side. A dozen or more perches made of quarter-inch dowels can be easily drilled into the sides and glued in place. A few tiny air holes near the tops of the sides will complete this shelter.

4

I think again about eight-tenths of one cent per bird per day and conclude that this is an infinitesimal amount of money to pay for such worthwhile entertainment, learning, and music. And it is small payment for the great service rendered by the birds in controlling insects and other pests throughout the year in our area.

Angels From The North

Unusually cold air masses from the Arctic have brought about some pleasant and unpleasant bird experiences. Earlier in December, I had been a bit too hasty in attributing the total absence of evening grosbeaks to the colder-than-usual weather systems, figuring that the birds had been induced to fly farther south.

Finally, in early January, a friend reported about 9 evening grosbeaks at his feeders. A week ago Clayton Moegenburg asked about the gray, robin-sized, long-tailed birds that were eating the seeds on the white ash trees near the Sandpiper Restaurant. They turned out to be pine grosbeaks. Yesterday morning, January 15, Sis Leino called from Kinsey Bay at 7:50 A.M., all excited, to report a flock of evening grosbeaks at her feeders. Ten minutes later, 16 of the sunflower-seed-eating champions appeared very much at home on our feeding platforms. This morning their number is up to 30. They have arrived at last!

The evening grosbeaks rarely miss spending part of each winter in Door County. Pine grosbeaks, on the other hand, are more likely to be winter visitors no oftener than once every five or six years. These strictly tree-dwelling birds are holarctic in their distribution; that is, they are native to the northern parts of both the Old and New Worlds. People of northern Japan, Siberia, Russia, and Scandinavia know this bird as well as do Canadians and Alaskans.

Its genus name, *Pinicola,* indicates that the pine grosbeak inhabits pine woods. *Enucleator,* its species name, reflects its skill at extracting kernels from seeds of all kinds, including some inside fruits such as apples. In fact, this is exactly what I saw them doing as I returned from the post office yesterday morning. For a week or more now, they have been favoring a small white ash tree laden with slender winged seeds, near the junction of Ridges Drive and Highway 57.

Even though the temperature was 10 below zero F., I decided to try getting some photographs of these erratic wanderers. But by the time I

Charlotte Lukes

Pine Grosbeak

got my cameras, lenses, filters, and tripod organized, then packed into the car, the birds had left the tree. However, with the effort I had put into this frigid venture, I wasn't about to give up that easily, and so, I parked the car in front of the snowbank along the highway north of the village and got out to listen and watch.

My hunch paid off. Several far-carrying musical whistles, not unlike the lesser yellowlegs' calls in summer, came from near Walter Zahn's house on the corner. "TEE-TEE-tew, TEE-TEE-tew." Over and over they called, directing my attention to their whereabouts— several in a small flowering crabapple tree, about 10 feeding in one of the white ash trees, and a few perched in the tall arborvitae trees. Thoreau described their song as having "dazzling beauty," these "angels from the north."

Much to my delight, they lived up to their reputation for being unusually tame. In fact, they are almost stupidly tame. I slowly eased through a foot of snow, carrying my camera gear, until I was within close range of them. From there I managed to snap several pictures of these social singers gulping down one after another tiny crabapple or ash seed.

After watching the little gluttons gorge themselves, I decided to take a few clusters of seedlings home with me, not only to identify them, but also to taste them for myself. The average white ash seed is one-and-a-half inches long, including the wing. The kernel is about one-half inch in length, long and slender, and like a grain of wild rice. It is mildly bitter to the taste, but very mealy and chewable.

The pine grosbeak is the largest of the grosbeaks, about one inch longer than the familiar evening grosbeak. Its long black tail gives it the edge in length. It has narrow white wing bars, a stubby heavy dark bill and, in general, is a grayish, robin-sized bird. The young, which are gray like the adult females, nearly always outnumber the adults of their species. Young males sometimes exhibit rusty to brassy-orange rump patches and have the same coloring on the backs of their heads. Both young and old females show a more or less light yellowish-olive coloring on their rumps and backs.

Three or four of the flock of about 20 were adult males, easy to distinguish because of the dull pinkish-red color of their heads, backs, and breasts. Their feathers have gray bases and, consequently, a few of the males appeared more gray than red.

Pine grosbeaks spend most winters within their Canadian breeding

range; only during winters of severe food shortages do they migrate farther south. They tend to be very gregarious at this time as they search
out their favorite foods—the seeds of pine, beech, ash, mountain ash,
highbush, cranberry, crabapple (a special favorite), sumac, red cedar,
blackberry, snowberry, maple, shadblow, juniper, and lilac.

Circumpolar nesters in the edges of the pine-spruce-fir belt, these
birds of the remote wilderness have not learned to fear man. Their
beauty and song help to temper the icy edge of Old Man Winter, and
anything you can do to help them will be well worth the effort. Read
over their favorite plant list, considering especially the white ash,
mountain ash, and the flowering crab. Plant them this summer near
your home so that by the next time the pine grosbeaks grace our winter
landscape—perhaps in another five or six years—plenty of natural food
will be available for them.

For the most part, we can do little or nothing to halt the steady increase in human population or the advance of technology, both of
which are responsible for the ruination of much of the natural landscape, plants, and animals. On the other hand if each family would
plant several food-producing trees and bushes attractive to the birds,
we could help them tremendously—and enjoy them at the same time!

Indispensable Raptors

Outside air temperature of 22 degrees below zero F., sharpened by a wind and laced with humidity off the lake, causes many people to wonder how birds and other wildlife can survive day after day, night after night. That they do survive is testimony to the marvelous insulating qualities of fur, feathers and down.

It was obviously the deadly cold temperature, accompanied by a wind-chill factor of minus 37 degrees F., that caused the cardinals to be about 90 minutes later than usual in their breakfast arrival at the feeders. The chickadees came in first at 8 A.M., followed by the goldfinches and purple finches 10 minutes later, and several cardinals 5 minutes after the finches. Each cardinal had a beautiful little ribbon of ice crystals above its eyes—on its eyebrows, so to speak. When we saw small puffs of frozen water vapor come from their mouths as they fed, we could understand the formation of this hoarfrost.

A quick estimate, counting by tens, indicated about 100 finches, most of them goldfinches, feeding outside the north kitchen window. It was a scene somewhat like this that led to an interesting experience a few days ago at the home of Matt McOlash, near Gills Rock. The McOlashes had been surprised by the sound of a loud ''thud'' against their living room window, it seemed to shake the house. When they ran to see what had happened, they found in the snow, on the ground beneath the window, a large hawk. Apparently it had made a pass at the finches, missed, and crashed into the window. There it lay, quivering and injured.

Charlotte and I were unable to drive up to Gills Rock until later the following afternoon. It was then we learned that the injured hawk had roosted during the night on a low branch of a small cedar tree, unable to fly.

At the time we arrived, the McOlashes had not seen the hawk for a couple of hours and thought it had flown away. Nevertheless, we decided to walk along the road and search the woods for it. In less than a minute I saw a dark form flapping toward a neighbor's woodpile.

Charlotte went around one side of the woodpile, and I—carrying a large fish-landing net—went around the other. There we discovered the bird, an immature goshawk, flailing at the snow with its wings in an attempt to escape. It was a simple matter for me to capture it.

Cautiously, I picked it up with both hands, taking great care to stay clear of its powerful talons, and placed it in a large wire cage Matt loaned us, and we were soon on our way back to Baileys Harbor—Charlotte, the goshawk, and I. It was nearly dark by the time we arrived home. The weather report was for another night of sub-zero conditions so we put the injured creature in the basement, where it would be warm and dark, and then went upstairs. Suddenly the oil furnace "kicked in," and the goshawk let out a piercing scream. Naturally it was frightened, but that was the first and last time it screamed. When Charlotte quietly checked on the bird later, she found that it had tucked its head under a wing and was fast asleep. Were we relieved!

After discussing what to do with the bird, we decided to call Ty Baumann, manager of the Bay Beach Wildlife Sanctuary, north of Green Bay. He told us they had a good caged pen in which to care for the young goshawk and also plenty of live white rats and roadkills, such as cottontails, which they have found to be a good diet for their captive raptors.

The injured bird appeared to be strong and peppy as Ty's young assistant removed it from the wire cage. A small amount of dried blood near its nostrils clearly indicated that it had received a hard blow to the head when it flew into the window. Mr. Baumann assured me that even though the bird might have suffered a concussion and was still in a slight state of shock and paralysis, it was strong and most likely would recover soon. It would then be returned to the wild.

Imagine our joy that night, after returning from the wildlife sanctuary, to see a beautiful advertisement on television sponsored by the U. S. Fish and Wildlife Service, reminding viewers that all eagles, hawks, and owls are protected by law, and that they are vital links in helping maintain a healthy population and balance of other wild animals and birds. As we thought about the phone call from the McOlashes, the trip to Gills Rock, the night of "hawk sitting," and the ride to Green Bay to deliver the goshawk to the sanctuary we were pleased that we had been able to help save a predatory bird that at one time was considered to be one of the most destructive birds in the country. How times have changed!

Cheery Wild Canary

A certain feeling in the air yesterday morning signaled a change in the weather. Whatever that something was, it moved me into action. I split several days' supply of kindling and filled all the woodboxes in the house.

Around noon, bird activity at the feeders was unusually heavy. And then it began—a slow, heavy, wet snow.

Out of the east it came, carrying with it excessive moisture from off the lake. At about 3:45, just before dark, I went out to clean off all the feeders, as well as the ground beneath them. One by one the cardinals came, as they always do before dark, to have their last food for the day. At one point, 12 were feeding.

On into the night the snow fell, and the barometer slowly slid downward. My alarm clock chased me out of the ''sack'' at 5 this morning to find the evergreens weighted to the extreme with heavy snow. Their lower branches embraced the ground, and even a few of the long branches of one of the maple trees were touching bottom. I had to push a considerable amount of snow out of the way with the kitchen door before I could open it. One shovelful of the white stuff brought back memories of the farm and shoveling fresh manure—heavy! Yikes, it was heavy!

It took me nearly an hour to clean the paths to the woodshed, the garage, and the feeding areas. Just before I finished, and noticed the eastern sky beginning to show light, I heard first one ''chip,'' then another, and another. Quickly, I scattered a pail of sunflower seeds on the ground and onto all the platform feeders, and then went into the house and pressed my nose to the window.

Within a minute or so they began to move in—the cardinals. Soon all 12 were quite peacefully having breakfast. I breathed a bit easier, knowing that the storm hadn't claimed any of them.

Chickadees flew in next, then the purple finches. Last to move in were the evening grosbeaks. The highest count was 30 finches and 40 grosbeaks, all getting along together remarkably well on the large platform feeders. Seems as though they sense hardship, in this case the storm, and are much more tolerant of one another than on a normal day.

Soon as breakfast was finished, I started shoveling the snow from the driveway. I was quite amazed at how closely the purple finches allowed me to approach before they flew up to the maple tree branches. I started at the road and moved downhill toward the garage as I usually do when the snow is deep. A large flock of goldfinches came sweeping in several times giving forth with their friendly cheeEE, cheeEE, cheeEE call as they flew. There must have been about 75 of them. Apparently the activity and chatter of the other feeding birds had lured them down, for soon they too were feasting on sunflower seeds.

Many people do not realize that the American goldfinches, commonly referred to as wild canaries, are with us year-round and that they do not generally migrate southward as do most of our other summer nesting birds. The fact that the male goldfinch molts in the fall of the year, changing from his brilliant black and yellow plumage to the delicate olive-gray color of the female, leads most folks to believe that they have left the area. As many finches do during the winter season, they gather into quite sizable flocks, frequently associating—apparently on very friendly terms—with redpolls and tree sparrows.

Bradford Torrey, in 1885, wrote a beautiful description of the American goldfinch. "Our American goldfinch is one of the loveliest of birds. With his elegant plumage, his rhythmical, undulatory flight, his beautiful song, and his more beautiful soul, he ought to be one of the best beloved, if not one of the most famous; but he has never yet had half his desserts. He is like the chickadee, and yet different. He is not so extremely confiding, nor should I call him merry. But he is always cheerful, in spite of his so-called plaintive note from which he gets one of his names, and always amiable. So far as I know, he never utters a harsh sound; even the young ones, asking for food, use only smooth, musical tones. During the pairing season his delight often becomes rapturous. To see him then, hovering and singing—or, better still, to see the devoted pair hovering together, billing and singing—is enough to do even a cynic good."

Indeed, their visit and songs this morning melted my cynicism toward the snow to be shoveled. And a good thing, too, because it wasn't long before it was all "re-piled" and I was ready for more!

13

Golden Featherweight

Here in the north country, I live for the day in January when the sky clears, the wind calms, and several subtle hints of spring can be detected. The mere fact that each day has a few more minutes of sunlight than the previous day gives me added optimism.

We received our favorite introduction to spring January 12, as we skied out to Toft's Point with our friends Jim and Libby Zimmerman. The cold stillness of the early afternoon was suddenly interrupted by five or six low sonorous hoots of a great horned owl concealed somewhere nearby in the dense evergreen trees. The low "love call" was quickly answered by a considerably higher hooting reply. After several minutes of silence, we heard another low song followed again by the high. This is the owls' prelude to mating and nesting, which may be in progress as early as the middle part of February.

A short while later our outing took us past a grove of large white spruces whose lower branches rested on the ground. Suddenly two small birds came into view, very active, flitting on their wing tips, nearly helicopter-like in manner, searching among the needles for insect food. My first thought was—chickadee. Charlotte, who was in the lead, got a close look at the birds and happily shouted back, "Golden-crowned kinglets!"

Peaceable and confiding, these diminutive gleaners actually appeared to float instead of fly. There was no swooping or dipping to their flight. Their extremely fast wing beats gave us the impression that they glided in short spurts from branch to branch.

Birders in past years have recorded nesting golden-crowned kinglets in Door County as well as other northern Wisconsin counties. It is not uncommon for these amazing creatures to winter in the vicinity of their previous summer nesting haunts, usually in the spruce, hemlock, balsam fir, and tamarack woods. I have seen them here several times in past winters, most often in the company of black-capped chickadees and a few times with brown creepers.

14

Charlotte Lukes

Golden-Crowned Kinglet

There are also a few records of ruby-crowned kinglets wintering this far north. This species is distinguished by its light eye-ring, while the golden-crowned has two light wing bars, as well as the white stripe over the eye, bordered by a black stripe. A close look will reveal the golden crown patch or, less often, the ruby-colored "top knot."

Migration of the golden-crowned kinglets usually is inconspicuous, because they tend to winter so far north. One of my most memorable bird sightings involved these carefree acrobats. I was on my way to teach at a school in Shorewood Hills, near Madison, one morning in late fall and was driving along the road bordering the south shore at Lake Mendota. It was extremely windy, and waves were nearly washing onto the road. Suddenly I saw dozens of small birds catching insects on the road. I stopped my car, got out, and slowly walked ahead to determine what they were. Imagine my surprise when I discovered myself surrounded by perhaps 500 or more unsuspicious, happy-hearted golden-crowned kinglets. To this day I cannot imagine how I managed to arrive at school on time!

A golden-crowned kinglet is also the subject of one of my favorite photographs. I was doing some spring bird-banding with Tom Erdman on Point Sauble, north of Green Bay, along the east shore. John Zoerb, of LaCrosse, and another friend had come along for the experience and to take some pictures. One of the many birds we banded that morning was a female golden-crowned kinglet. I had her nestled in one hand and was gently grasping her right leg between my thumb and the tip of my index finger. The photograph shows her peeking out from the half-dollar-size opening of my fingers. How tiny she was!

We think back in awe at the size-comparison between our two star performers last week at the Point. The 3½-inch-long kinglet weighs about .18 of one ounce. Eighty-eight of them would equal one pound! How can this tiny bird withstand a wind-chill factor of 60 degrees below zero?

The great horned owl, by contrast, averages about 3½ pounds and is approximately 18 inches long. Its wingspan of 54 inches compares with the kinglet's 7-inch span. The burly great horned owls—flying tigers—300 times heavier than the petite kinglets, sang their early spring song. And the kinglets, like over sized bumblebees, went about their serious business of finding insect eggs, proving to us that they could survive sub-zero weather in spite of their size. All in all, these two extremes of birds made us feel good all over, convinced that we would withstand the remainder of winter.

Flaming Foreheads

January 31 was a red-letter day, or perhaps I should say a red-forehead day, for on that date the redpolls arrived at our feeders! Just about the time everyone is asking, "Where are all the birds this winter," and I'm replying, "Be patient, give them time," here they are. The minute these classy, common redpolls make their appearance, all the other species at the feeders are of secondary importance.

Undoubtedly it is their irregular and unpredictable appearance that makes these spirited visitors so welcome. They are circumpolar wanderers of the first magnitude. A redpoll that was trapped and banded in Michigan one spring was recaptured by a Russian ornithologist the following spring in Siberia, nearly 4,000 miles away!

These stubby-billed finches, about the size of the chickadee, have three facial characteristics that are easy to see: a red cap, a yellow bill, and a black chin spot. Their upper parts are streaked with brown, making them appear similar to pine siskins from a distance. The species name of the common redpolls is *flammea*, an allusion to the red forehead patch and also to the beautiful rosy pink that dribbles down the breast of the male. My wife says that their forehead patches are American Beauty rose in color.

Redpolls, along with goldfinches, evening grosbeaks, and pine siskins, belong to a subfamily of the huge finch family—the *carduelines*, a name that derives from a genus of thistles, *Carduus*, that these birds favor. They also use the thistle down in their nests. The carduelines are inhabitants of the northern forest and its immediate edges. It is common for them to sing while in their spectacular undulating flight. All are highly social, particularly in winter, when the availability of food triggers their free-wheeling, wide-ranging movements. However, none of the carduelines is strongly migratory, and it is uncommon for them to travel south of the 40th parallel.

As my wife and I and a friend were returning from an afternoon of cross-country skiing at Newport State Park about two weeks ago, we spotted a large flock of redpolls feeding on weed seeds along Timberline Road. The neat rows of the last summer's stalks of pigweed indicated that a garden had been planted there. What the owners didn't realize was that one of their unwanted, unharvested crops would, come January, help to feed this scintillating company of redpolls.

Early colonists in America recognized redpolls because these birds also inhabited their home countries in Europe. I am sure that the redpolls consumed much of the same food in winter then as they do now, the bulk of it consisting of the seeds of birch, alder, willow, ragweed, smartweed, and pigweed. Their summer diet also includes many small insects.

I'll always remember the first flock of common redpolls I saw. It was back in January of 1960. I had been counting bald eagles most of the day along the open flowage below the Petenwell Dam on the Wisconsin River, south of Wisconsin Rapids. Luckily, I decided to warm up in the generating plant late in the afternoon. There, intent upon finding weed seeds on the southwest back of the earthen dam, a very sociable, tolerant flock of about 150 common redpolls entertained me for about 15 minutes.

A couple of years later, in March, I was visiting with my friends, the Hunters, west of Green Bay. That spring I banded more than 500 purple finches in their yard, and it had been a memorable season for large numbers of birds. As usual, Hy and I were up well before daybreak to nurse steaming mugs of coffee and watch for the first hint of morning down through the woods to the east.

Suddenly we detected a movement of birds out in the 20-acre field beyond the woods. The more intently we watched, the larger the flock appeared. Finally, the temptation to have a closer look overcame us and we went out. A multitude of weeds showed above the snow and it was upon these that the flock was feasting—redpolls, hundreds of them!

Much to our surprise and utter enjoyment, the flock—safe in its great size—ignored us as we inched our way into its midst. We turned ever so slowly, counting, estimating all the while. Our final figure was between three and four thousand. Surely it was a once-in-a-lifetime experience.

17

Dreaming Of Spring

The pleasantly sunny warm weather of the past weekend made us appreciate our part of the country more than ever, especially in light of the dreadful West Coast storms and the equally awful ''digging-out'' operations in the East. Now comes a 30-day forecast of cold temperatures which prompts me to take out last year's phenology (natural phenomena) book. I simply must convince myself by reference to actual previous records that spring is just around the snowbank.

Horned larks, those fearless champions of spring, were seen along the roadsides by early February. The first robin and red-winged blackbird visited the backyard in preparation for the coming season on March 12. The next day the first chipmunk braved the chilly morning and emerged from his burrow beneath the woodpile. He appeared very agile, a marvelous feat considering that he had been confined to his dark, cramped quarters for more than five months.

Slate-colored juncos were scratching among the sunflower seed hulls at sunrise on the 14th, while three ruffed grouse ate the swelled buds of the quaking aspens within 50 feet of the kitchen. Grackles, the next day, proved that they had not lost their pompous strutting technique and that the male's glossy purple-and-bronze head and neck were as beautiful as they were last year. Meadowlarks were sighted two days later near Art Stieglitz's farm, west of town.

March 19th—the first killdeeer teetered along the open shoulders of the road against a backdrop of waning snowbanks. A week later, on the 26th, Olivia Traven called, all excited, to tell of a small group of cedar waxwings feasting on the fruits of her highbush cranberry shrubs. At first she thought they were Bohemian waxwings and that she was really going to please this Bohemian bird-watcher!

Juncos appeared to reach their peak numbers by March 28. We watched hundreds of them along the grassy roadsides, searching for weed seeds as they slowly followed spring northward with a wary eye. The much-awaited male woodcock sang his first aerial aria on the evening of the 29th. Earlier that day, we had watched the first brown creepers spiraling the maple trees, always from the ground upward, seeking insect eggs that the chickadees and nuthatches missed during the winter.

Catkins on the aspens were noticeably enlarged by March 30, when the song sparrow arrived and immediately launched into his robust, sneezy, wheezy, sputtery, hiccup-like song. Hooded mergansers, buffleheads, and common mergansers, confined to the 100-yard-long opening south of the causeway on icebound Kangaroo Lake, ended our list of newcomers for the month of March.

There was no fooling on April 1: The large gray hawk with the tippy flight and obvious white rump-patch was a harrier, commonly referred to as the marsh hawk. The first fox sparrows of the year arrived at the feeders on April 4, just in the nick of time. For a genuine, old-fashioned blizzard (Do you remember them?) set in during the afternoon; and by morning, 13½ inches of wet, lead-heavy snow greeted us and our snow shovels. But along with the white stuff came a delightful roll call of birds in search of food in the backyard: fox sparrow, tree sparrow, junco, robin, evening grosbeak, purple finch, goldfinch, cardinal, red-breasted nuthatch, chickadee, blue jay, red-winged blackbird, grackle, starling, downy woodpecker—16 hungry species in all. Later that day, while out to inspect the effects of the blizzard, we added to our list the redhead duck, pied-billed grebe, and kingfisher—all seen at Kangaroo Lake.

A male rufous-sided towhee scratched with great vigor beneath the white spruces out in the backyard on April 8 in search of insects and seeds. One spectacular male wood duck topped our list for the 9th; and two days later, while on her way to Sister Bay, Charlotte spotted a gopher along Highway 57.

April 11 was the warmest day of spring this far—73 degrees F. We were not surprised in the least to see our first butterfly of the year, an anglewing, drinking maple sap as it dripped from a broken twig on one of the big maples. Two great blue herons flew over later in the day. The unusually warm temperature lured us out in the evening, and we drove down to the little marsh bordering Hibbard's Creek, just east of Bill Honald's farm, to listen to the season's first concert, performed by myriad spring peepers, wood frogs, and western chorus frogs.

We counted a high of 16 fox sparrows at the feeders on April 12. The next day a "kettle" of broad-winged hawks lazily floated high over the Sanctuary. Ruth Neuman called on April 13, thrilled to report the first barn swallow. Later that day tree swallows and blue-winged teal were added to our list. On a visit that afternoon to Walter and Bertha Reinhard's woods, we saw our first blooming hepaticas.

Both the ruby-crowned and golden-crowned kinglets behaved as though they were official twig inspectors in the yard on April 15, as they scrutinized every nook and cranny in the bark. The first catkins opened on the aspens that day, and the pine siskins and evening grosbeaks continued to gobble down the sunflower seeds. We were beginning to think these birds would remain here all summer. And then, our thrill of thrills was also seen on the 15th: our first eastern bluebird at one of our favorite spots, Bluebird Corner, near Walter Green's!

On our way to Reinhard's woods we saw whistling swans, white-throated sparrows, a common snipe, shoveler ducks, yellow-bellied sap-suckers, and a vesper sparrow. Once there, we enjoyed our first moosewood (shrub) and bloodroot flowers of the early spring.

I guess I had better stop reminiscing or else summer will be half over before it even arrives. I strongly recommend that you begin a yearly phenology list. It will sharpen your awareness of the natural world around you and especially will give you a basis for recognizing the continuous change that is part of the excitement of natural phenomena. Happy spring—although my records of last year indicate we had better keep our snow shovels handy for awhile!

Night Hunters

Few birds have been more admired throughout history than those priceless wonders designed for darkness, the owls. Their distinctive beauty and alert upright stance, coupled with their people-like flat faces, obviously fascinate us.

Look around. Chances are that an owl peers down at you in some form of art; or perhaps it takes the form of a toy, a stuffed pillow, or a piece of jewelry. A life-sized, painted plastic model of a handsome screech owl stares at me from its perch alongside one of the bookshelves here in my study. And my dad's Uncle Wodsadalek's beautiful carving of a tiny owl, species unknown, stands on the old walnut table by the living-room window.

A tawny-feathered ceramic owl decorates the entrance to the kitchen doorway, courtesy of my art teacher friend, Mrs. Thiry. A little owl cup sits on the window ledge, and a picture of Audubon's famous snowy owls, perched in a dead tree on a moonlight night, hangs next to the Franklin stove. They complete our owl collection.

Don't be fooled by the owl's docile, feathery, short, squat appearance. I received a surprise several years ago when a neighbor brought in a dead barred owl that he had found next to his garage. After examining and photographing the bird, I decided to prepare a "study skull" and as part of the process, I plucked the head clean. How long and flexible its neck was in proportion to its large head!

Although engaging in appearance, owls are well equipped for the predatory life they live. Powerful, wide feet and pointed talons are camouflaged beneath beautiful feathers. And a strong, hooked, downward-pointing bill can barely be seen.

Upon examining the ears of an owl, you will be interested to find that the ear flaps are in front of the exceptionally large auditory openings. The extreme width (for so small an animal) between the two ears enables owls to detect a time lapse of three ten-thousandths of one second, thus making it possible for them to tell whether a sound is made to the left or right of a certain point. Tests have proven that even in total darkness, owls can zero in with deadly accuracy on prey that has made a noise in its movements. Their shallow sunken facial discs are believed to act as parabolic reflectors in concentrating faint sounds into a smaller, concise area of acute hearing.

These little-known and frequently misunderstood creatures have unusually large eyes in proportion to their body size. For example, a snowy owl (about two feet long) has eyes nearly as large as an adult human's! Positioned at the front of the head, they give the bird binocular vision, unlike that of other birds. Owls, like people, have overlapping sight. An arc of about 70 degrees of their 110-degree vision is seen by both eyes. This characteristic enhances their ability to judge distance accurately and is vital to their survival.

Ornithologists believe that owls' flight feathers, fringed at their edges and covered with a very short velvety pile, enable them to fly silently to avoid scaring off their prey. Very likely this adaptation also cuts down on flight-wind noise against their feathers, enabling them to hear their prey better.

Of the 133 species of owls in the world, only 6 are considered to be fairly common nesters in Wisconsin—the great horned, barred, long-eared, short-eared, screech, and saw-whet. Snowy owls, from the great northern tundra, are fairly common winter visitors in some years. Occasionally, a great gray, barn, boreal, hawk (owl), and even a burrowing owl will show up in Wisconsin.

Several years ago a saw-whet owl, found killed against a fence of small chicken wire on a farm, was brought to school by one of my students. This miniature seven-inch owl looked like a child's stuffed toy. Bernard Brouchoud has banded many saw-whets during their fall migratory flight near the Lake Michigan shore between Manitowoc and Two Rivers.

It was a very happy day a few years ago, when the great horned owls of Wisconsin, flying tigers of the nighttime skies, were added to the list of protected birds. Now, fortunately, all owls, as well as other birds of prey, can rest in safety (at least legally) from trigger-happy hunters.

Soon the songs of owls will be added to the soft sonorous edge of the singing winds of spring nights, long before the whippoorwills arrive to add their tremulous voices to the nocturnal concert.

Man has only recently begun to understand the important role of owls in nature. Protecting, preserving, and encouraging our owl

Charlotte
Lukes

Saw-Whet Owl

population by providing nesting boxes will not only benefit man in numerous ways, but will strengthen his understanding of his own place in the great Web of Life.

The Shy Westerner

A state record may be set during this winter of 1977-78 for the numbers of an unusually rare and beautiful bird being seen in various parts of Wisconsin, but especially in the eastern part. The bird is the varied thrush.

Individual sightings have been made in seven different localities: Appleton, Clintonville, Chippewa Falls, Haven (north of Sheboygan), Briggsville (east of Wisconsin Dells), Sister Bay, and Sand Bay (northeastern Door County). The two seen in Door County, both males, are coming to backyard feeding stations that are several miles apart and are definitely two different birds.

About 50 varied thrushes have been recorded in Wisconsin through past years, ranging back to the first recorded sighting, which occurred in Madison in 1944. They have been known to arrive as early as October and depart as late as the third week in April. Several have continued to come daily to feeding stations for as long as four months.

Their breeding range extends from Alaska and the Mackenzie Territory of Canada south to Washington and western Montana. Those wintering in Door County may have flown over an easterly route of approximately 1,500 to 1,800 miles.

Owen Gromme, in his book, *Birds of Wisconsin*, lists this classy bird as an accidental visitor to this state, along with such others as the green-tailed towhee, scissor-tailed flycatcher, and the mountain bluebird. It is difficult to say why this bird, native to the coniferous woodlands of the Pacific Northwest and Alaska, occasionally appears far to the east of its home territory.

The very reasons why birds migrate is an interesting subject to study. Surely severe winters, the need to locate food, and a search for breeding sites are important factors. Research has shown that bobolinks, pectoral sandpipers, purple finches, and evening grosbeaks are known to make easterly and westerly flights during the course of their yearly migrations. Evening grosbeaks and purple finches banded

24

in northern Michigan were retrapped in several of the eastern Atlantic states. I continue to be amazed by the purple finch I banded near here, which was recovered in Prince George, British Columbia 63 days later—a distance of about 1,800 miles!

One quite interesting theory of bird migration contends that some migratory routes have been established according to climate changes that followed the retreat of the last glacier, within the past 10,000 years. One can easily imagine the changes of vegetation—the source of many birds' food—that occurred as the ice slowly melted.

Could these varied thrushes have become lost—perhaps associated with a flock of grosbeaks, finches, or robins—and, driven by the advancing fingers of a snowstorm, landed in this western Lake Michigan region? Perhaps it is essentially because of the effect of the prevailing westerly winds. If this were the explanation, however, why wouldn't more of these birds be seen here?

People in the West have several names for the varied thrush, including Oregon robin, banded robin, Alaska robin, and Pacific varied thrush. Strangely, inasmuch as it resembles the American robin, it has an entirely different genus name: *Ixoreus*, which means mistletoe-berry-mountain. One can only guess that somebody a long time ago associated these thrushes with either eating mistletoe berries or living in mountainous regions—or both!

In checking the range map in Robbins' book, *Birds of North America*, you will find that the varied thrush breeds from northern California into northern Alaska and northwestern Canada. Varied thrushes are present in winter in about half of their breeding range, extending from southern California north into Washington and southern Alaska.

They tend to favor firs, hemlocks, and cedars—dark, shady, humid evergreen stands. Their nesting habitat appears to require shade, coolness, and dampness—laced with fog and frequent rains. It is said that the varied thrush needs rain almost as a fish needs water. Perhaps this helps to account for these accidental visitors' apparent success in wintering near Lake Michigan or Green Bay.

The widely distributed thrush family, to which this bird belongs, includes about 150 species, which nest in North and South America. They tend to have strong legs, are powerful fliers, and, above all, are beautiful singers. Only four thrushes nest in our part of Wisconsin, the veery, wood thrush, American robin, and eastern bluebird. From the few times I have seen them, I would say varied thrushes are very shy and elusive, somewhat like the veery and wood thrush.

The varied thrush's double toned, ethereal song reminds me of the wood thrush and, even more so, the veery. One recording I made of a veery, when played back at a slower speed, lowers the song two octaves in pitch and clearly reveals the double-toned nature of the singing. In fact, this bird definitely sings up and down the scale at the same time!

People who have heard the varied thrush sing—a thrilling experience on mild, foggy mornings—say that its mysterious and melancholy voice matches the peaceful, secluded solitude in which the bird chooses to live.

Lately, I have been wondering whether these strangers to Door County will find their way home. Do they have homing ability? Can they use the sun or other forms of stellar navigation to find their way? Or perhaps they respond to polarized light or have something amounting to memory that enables them to retrace their easterly flight of several months ago.

Having come to know a tiny bit about these elegant birds, we have resolved to locate them if we ever have the opportunity to be in Seattle, Washington, in late May. But until that trip becomes a reality, these unusual ''accidentals'' will have to suffice. Welcome to Door County, rare visitors!

Crimson-Crowned Aristocrat

One of the most highly specialized avian ''tree surgeons'' greeted me in the forest yesterday. It was the pileated woodpecker. Its loud harsh calls, ''CUDuk-CUDuk-CUDuk,'' echoed high above the wooded bluffs. A neighbor from up the road had called with excitement the day before to report seeing one in his backyard, and to remark on how large this crow-sized creature was.

I don't know of another bird that creates as much excitement and awe every time it is seen as this splendid aristocrat, decked out in his suit of bold black and white feathers, and highlighted by a blazing crimson crown. Perhaps it is because they are such shy loners and require large territories that each sighting is so memorable.

The bird I saw was a very inquisitive female. Her loud cries immediately revealed her presence. Unafraid, she flew to the highest branches of a nearby beech tree. There, the late afternoon sun backlighted her flaming headdress as she eyed me with apparent curiosity. Her jerky movements and occasional banging on a dead twig seemed to reflect nervousness more than any serious attempt at food-finding. Soon she circled and flew directly overhead, her strong wing beats in perfect time to her calls, ''CUDuk-CUDuk-CUDuk.''

The imposing pileated woodpeckers seem to have a strong preference for particular habitats, and thus, they are uncommon throughout much of their range. Their usual habitat includes mature woodlands that still have some standing dead trees. The eastern half of the U. S. and the southern half of Canada, except for parts of the prairie provinces in the west, list pileated woodpeckers as permanent residents. Birders consider themselves fortunate if, during a lifetime, they see even a few of these beautiful birds.

Dying or dead trees are important to the pileated woodpeckers' survival. Carpenter ants and other wood-boring insects, such as horntails, very likely caused the death of the tree in the first place; now it is they that the ''tree surgeons'' are in search of. Powerful hammering blows by their straight, hard, chisel-like bills help them to reach their food quickly. It is thought that the vibrations of the insects, or possibly the strong odor of formic acid given off by the carpenter ants, serves as the targets at which "Piley" aims his attack. The barbed tongue tip, coated with a sticky substance, is thought to be highly alkaline, perfect for neutralizing the strong formic acid.

Its short, strong legs; curved, needle-sharp claws; thick, shock-absorbent skull; and stiff tail feathers (used as a prop against a tree) all serve this wily bird well. Surprisingly, many of its excavations made in quest of food are rectangular in shape. In watching it work I have found that a common technique is for the bird to chisel a four- or five-inch sliver of wood loose, grasp it with its beak, and pull it off the tree. These actions result in long, rectangular holes.

These stately creatures do very well in winter. They excavate a special winter shelter and occasionally even enjoy the luxury of locating a concealed ant colony, where the dormant, slow-moving insects become easy prey.

One of my most interesting observations of a pileated woodpecker took place at Toft's Point several winters ago. I could hear a woodpecker working ahead as I quietly snowshoed toward the buildings. Finally I spied "Piley" working near the base of a large arborvitae tree. Apparently the meal was too good to abandon just because I had arrived on the scene, so I was able to watch him for two or three minutes from within 40 feet. Then came the surprise. The woodpecker, probably now grown impatient with my presence, flew into the woods. Within seconds a couple of black-capped chickadees, a red-breasted nuthatch, and a downy woodpecker—the "clean-up crew"—took over where Piley left off. What a thorough going-over the dinner table received! Not a single crumb was wasted as these efficient gleaners went about their work.

Ever since this incident, I have noticed many times while using an ax or hammer in the woods, that my pounding invariably attracted several small birds, especially chickadees. Undoubtedly they were conditioned by the distant pounding of Piley, working to get his next meal, to believe that he might leave a few scraps behind for them. I have indeed been flattered to think that I sounded like a pileated woodpecker!

The Bird Of Merry Heart

Did you ever lay eyes on a ''sad'' chickadee? Chances are all answers will be no. Bradford Torrey, back in the 1890s, knew that answer when he described this well-known bird as ''the bird of merry heart.'' For that reason, I can't think of a more fitting remedy for the February ''blahs'' than watching these boldly marked, amiable little squirts.

Several weeks had slipped by since any of the beady-eyed midgets had fed from my hands. Finally, the perfect opportunity arose last week, when I skied out to Toft's Point to tend to the bird feeders. As expected, several chickadees were ready and eager for a handout. So instead of filling the feeders immediately, I did just that—held out both of my bare hands, each containing a couple dozen sunflower seeds.

Perhaps it was my old familiar red woolen cap they recognized and trusted, for within 30 seconds, the first confiding chickadee had taken a seed and retreated to the nearest branch in the spruce tree where he proceeded to get into the ''meat'' of the matter.

Almost every flock has one skeptical, untrusting individual, and this was no exception. The bird refused to take a seed even though some were already hulled. He would make a swerving pass, land within four or five feet, then scold incessantly with a rapid, high-pitched ''tsee-tsee-tsee-tsee.'' I followed his every move, to be sure. This was the bristling, impudent male who simply would not trust me.

I called him a male because I could detect an irregular bottom edge on his black chin patch. The same patch on the female is narrower beneath the beak and tends to be quite squared-off along the lower edge.

Finally, I put several seeds on the top of my cap and in a few moments enjoyed having as many as four chickadees perched on me at one instant. I marveled at how cold their feet were, the exact opposite of their outwardly warm, good natured actions.

Even though chickadees are regarded as permanent residents in many areas, more and more studies are indicating that there is a considerable departure from their northernmost breeding areas during the winter months. My own banding activities and general observations tend to indicate an increase in our own area from October through March.

Their normal range extends throughout much of the southern half of Canada south into northern California, New Mexico, Missouri, Ohio, North Carolina, and New Jersey. Occasionally, I get a report of a boreal chickadee being seen in this area. Their crowns are brown instead of black, and their flanks and backs are a deeper rust and brown.

I don't think people are nearly appreciative enough of the continuous onslaught these sharp-eyed acrobats wage against insects and their eggs. For even though they are regular customers at the suet feeder and sunflower-seed platform, they also spend a considerable part of each day in search of natural food, insects and insect eggs being among their favorites.

One black-capped chickadee gave me quite a surprise this morning, unexpected because of the below-zero weather. I was in the process of filling the wood boxes in the kitchen and study and was returning to the woodshed for another armful. Without thinking, in a happy mood, I let loose with my imitation of their high-pitched two-note whistle, HEEdee dee, HEEdee, dee, HEEdee, dee'' (the first note one full tone higher than the second; the second tone usually a double note). Back came an answer, much to my surprise. I'm not going to go so far as to try to interpret what that little scamp was saying, but it did leave me with a warm feeling toward that gentle but hardy black-bibbed ''buddy'' of mine.

Here I go rushing spring a bit, but it won't be too many weeks before these birds will be searching for nesting sites. Because they are cavity nesters, one of their favorite locations is a rather low, punky, decaying stump. In fact, I had a very sad experience several years ago with one of their nesting sites and learned from it a lesson I shall never forget.

I was returning home alone along Labrador Trail in the Ridges, when a chickadee flew across in front of me, no more than 10 feet away, directly to an old rotten pine stump situated among the Labrador Tea shrubs on the steep backslope of the ridge. I immediately sat down against a nearby tree to watch her busy activities to-and-from the nest. Finally, to satisfy my curiosity, I approached the stump very quietly and found that I could look down into the nest from the top to see six or seven beautiful little baby chickadees, only a few days from being ready to leave their secluded nursery.

The next day, in passing the chickadee's nest, I decided to have one more look. Imagine my horror when I found the rotten stump pulled apart and many chickadee feathers littering the ground. My guess is that either a skunk or a raccoon had followed my scent trail leading to the nest, ripped it apart, and eaten the birds. I still blame myself for the calamity. My lesson was learned the hard way. Ever since that misfortune I have stayed away from birds' nests, and I hope you will do the same.

One after another the chickadees buzz in for sunflower seeds, give me the once-over and tell me in their own way, "Chicka-dee-dee, keekee-kirk, keekee-kirk, dee-dee-dee," which interpreted means, "Get off your soft bottomside and come outdoors for some fresh air and exercise."

What Wonderful Eyes You Have!

In the cold pre-dawn darkness, Charlotte had a difficult time convincing me that it was I who had, the night before, told her to set the alarm clock for 5 A.M. I had scribbled avian ideas, experiences, words, and phrases on my scratch pad with the assumption that they would work on my subconscious mind as I slept. But to be honest, my dreams were far removed from birds.

I fumbled in the kitchen getting the coffee pot going, then inched the shade back for a peek at the thermometer. What a pleasant surprise to see it at zero degrees F., the warmest it has been at this early hour for days. The wind had calmed down, too, from a stinging 25 m.p.h. the night before.

These conditions, sub-zero cold and wind, make me recall one of the most gruesome, saddest experiences I ever had with birds. It happened in January 1973. That evening, as usual, Charlotte and I had watched the cardinals come in for their food at dusk. I distinctly recall the strong wind and the temperature of minus 4 degrees F. Come morning, when I went out to fill the feeders and scatter seeds on the ground as well, I noticed something dangling from the back of one of the aluminum and glass feeders.

When I reached the feeder, I was shocked to discover a male cardinal—frozen stiff, dead. He had reached into one of the holes, turned his head sideways and, accidentally, touched his left eye to the metal of the inside funnel. There, like an inquisitive boy touching his tongue to the icy cold pump handle of years ago, the cardinal was stuck fast. His struggles were in vain and he froze to death.

Even though the experts had told me this wouldn't happen, it did. The next day, I installed smooth, shiny, plastic-covered wire guards to prevent any recurrence.

I have often mentally reconstructed this event in an attempt to determine its cause. The strong wind throwing the bird off balance surely was a factor. Another possibility came to me last night as I was

Cardinal

reading *How To Talk To Birds*, written by Richard C. Davids and published by Alfred A. Knopf. In the book, Dr. Paul Fluck, a retired ophthalmologist from eastern Pennsylvania and one of the leading bird banders in the United States, says that it is fairly common for birds to have cataracts on the lenses of their eyes. In fact, he feels that this is what may prevent some birds from migrating south for the winter. Perhaps cataracts had reduced my unfortunate cardinal's vision.

Experts say that birds need superb eyesight for proper flight. In fact, birds' eyes are reported to be the most perfectly developed of any animal's, much larger in proportion to total body weight than man's. Several species of birds, including the largest of the owls, have eyeballs that are actually larger than our own. An owl such as this weighs about one-fiftieth as much as the average man. The larger size is certainly one indication of the importance of eyes to birds' survival.

Birds' eyes admit much more light and allow for a sharper image on the retina. In general, their marvelous eyes have about 100 times the light-gathering power of man's. And exceptional mobility of the iris allows their eyes to quickly adjust to dark and light conditions.

In addition to having two eyelids, birds possess a third, so-called nictitating membrane. It moves from the area of the beak outward, cleansing and lubricating the eyes and protecting them from injury.

Several years ago a neighbor called to tell me he had found a dead owl behind his garage. It turned out to be a very emaciated barred owl. In the process of preparing a ''study skull'' from it, I was quite amazed to discover that the eyeballs were not spherical as I had expected, but tubular and elongated. By comparing this eye to a telephoto lens, which has a long focal length, I realized how difficult it is for an owl to focus on nearby objects. I was reminded that every tme I had looked at a live owl in captivity, usually from very close range, the bird had slowly moved its head from side to side, thus helping it to focus on the strange creature staring at it.

We have constant reminders of the amazing eyesight of birds. Hummingbirds rapidly and precisely jab their long thin beaks through tiny openings in their feeders. Chickadees scrutinize branches, sometimes less than one inch from their eyes, for minute insect eggs. Evening grosbeaks cock their heads sideways as they munch on sunflower seeds, looking for the second seed even before they have finished the first.

But added to the beauty of birds eyes is the grim reminder—my hideous cardinal experience—of the extreme sensitivity of the organs. If you have the least doubt in mind as to the safety of your metal feeders, rub a piece of beef suet on those metal parts that may accidentally come into contact with their eyes. Those of us who feed birds every day must remember that their world is filled with natural hazards. Let's not be guilty of adding one more man-made hazard to that burden.

Your Favorite Bird

What makes a bird species become a particular favorite? Perhaps we can begin to answer this question by examining a list of the state birds. Topping them all is the cardinal; seven states chose it as their official bird. Next in line, with six choices, is the western meadowlark. Five states decided upon the mockingbird. And Wisconsin, Connecticut, and Michigan chose the robin.

I think it surprising to find that such common birds as the nuthatch, crow, owl, hawk, heron, jay, dove, swan, duck, blackbird, sparrow, warbler, hummingbird, and swallow were totally neglected. A fact that may shock some birders is that three states honor species that are not even native to the United States—Delaware, the blue hen chicken, and Rhode Island and South Dakota, the ring-necked pheasant (native of China)!

Many people ask me how the robin came to be the state bird of Wisconsin. School children throughout the state were called upon to make that decision. Surely the bird's widespread popularity is not to be denied. Look at the distribution map, a month-by-month representation of occurrences over 25 years or more, and you'll find that the robin has been seen in every county of this state during every month of the year.

But before you begin nodding your head in agreement saying, "See, I told you it was a good choice," consider this fact. The following birds, all natives, have also been observed in the wild during all months in every county: ruffed grouse, short-eared owl, screech owl, saw-whet owl, barred owl, great horned owl, downy woodpecker, hairy woodpecker, blue jay, black-capped chickadee, white-breasted nuthatch, cedar waxwing, cardinal, and American goldfinch. Suppose that the choice of our state bird was yours. Which of these, or others, would you choose? And this brings us back to my original question: Which factors influence the choice?

Here is another thought that may help you make up your mind. The following nine bird species enjoy the widest distribution of all native birds on this continent: screech owl, great horned owl, downy woodpecker, hairy woodpecker, horned lark, mourning dove, robin, white-breasted nuthatch, and common crow. Of these, which species inhabits the largest total area on the North American continent? I bet you'll be surprised to learn that the answer is the hairy woodpecker! But as handsome and economically important as the flashy woodpeckers are, only one has been chosen to represent a state—Alabamans decided upon the yellow-shafted flicker.

Now one of the points I'm trying to establish is this: It is extremely difficult to have one species of bird represent an entire state. I'm not at all against each state having its honored bird. But I would like to advocate that, in addition, each county adopt a county bird, as well as a county wildflower, tree, rock or mineral, butterfly, fish, mammal, etc., all chosen by school children.

I can't imagine a better way to introduce young people, as well as adults, to the native plants and animals of their county than by actively involving them in making intelligent choices. In the first place the students and their teachers would have to get to know what forms of life exist in their home areas. Well-thought-out guidelines would be a vital necessity in the final decision-making process. If all went well, both the students' awareness and respect for the natural environment would grow appreciably.

I like to think that a nation that has celebrated its 200th birthday should have instilled in its people, during those two centuries, great pride in knowing and understanding its natural history. Ideally, this learning should begin at the preschool level and continue throughout one's lifetime. Just think, if a student, by the time he or she graduates from high school, can't make a good choice for a county bird, wildflower, or tree, how could he or she be expected to be able to vote intelligently for our country's leaders?

Tiger of the Air

Some call him "Tiger of the Air." Scientists have tabbed him *Bubo virginianus*. But with all due respect to scientific nomenclature the great horned owl does deserve the unqualified title of TIGER.

For centuries owls were looked on with disdain by most people, and to a large extent they still are. Their unexpected eerie and mournful cries in the dark of night have frightened people out of their wits and caused them to dream up all sorts of ill-founded and idiotic superstitions about these grand creatures. The great horned owl, whose range extends from the northern tree limit of Canada clear down to the Strait of Magellan in South America, is a perfect owl species on which to base my "grand creature" description.

It is not uncommon to find "Mrs. Bubo" incubating eggs as early as mid-February here in Door County, snow sometimes circling the rim of the nest. Two or three white eggs are laid at several-day intervals and, unlike most other birds that wait until all eggs are laid before beginning to incubate them, she immediately begins incubating the first egg laid. A noticeable difference of development will be observed among the young as they mature. Some claim that the older of the fledglings will help to protect the smaller ones, while the parents are away from the nest.

Indeed, the great horned owl protects its nest viciously against intruders. A few years ago a pair of these birds established a nest in a small grove of evergreen trees near a sidewalk. On many occasions, the owls swooped down at people passing by, hoping to frighten them away and thus protect their young. Word spread rapidly and soon someone got the "brainstorm" that the owls were attacking because they were rabid. An expert archer was secured and he promptly shot both adult owls, little knowing that all the owls were doing was defending their nest.

The vision of the great horned owl is superb. And don't think for one second that it sees poorly in the daytime. Like any other creature with eyes, it sees much better during the day than at night. Its vision is binocular; both eyes are directed forward, much as human eyes are, giving the owl three-dimensional vision. Owls are most active during hours of darkness simply because that is the time when their prey is most active.

A fantastic experiment was conducted a few years ago to learn more about the power of owls' sight. Much to the experimenters' surprise, it was discovered that owls can locate and capture prey in total darkness. Here is how the study was done: Dried leaves were scattered over the floor at one end of a large empty shed. An owl was placed on a perch at the opposite end of the shed and the room was completely darkened. Then a mouse was released onto the leaf-covered floor. It scampered several feet and stopped. Immediately the owl launched itself, glided silently forward on down-covered wings, and seized the mouse. Unerringly it captured several mice in the same manner. When a crumpled piece of paper was dragged across the room in place of live prey, the owl struck the paper just as accurately.

Owls have comparatively large ears covered with bristly feathers and situated at the sides of their heads. Undoubtedly the owl in the experiment was using its ears to locate its prey. The ear flaps are arranged in a manner opposite to those of humans. The owl's flaps are directed toward the front of the head, and the openings into the ears are in back of the flaps.

The experimenters now took a large wad of cotton and carefully plugged one ear opening. Live prey was released, the owl launched itself—and missed! Depending upon which ear was plugged, the owl missed its mark by several feet either to the left or to the right. Thus, it became clear that as the prey moved across the ground, the owl slowly followed the sound by carefully turning its head so that each supersensitive ear picked up exactly the same volume of sound. As soon as the prey stopped, the owl was facing directly toward the prey. What a marvelous range finder!

The great horned owl can grow to be 18 to 25 inches in length, reach a weight of up to three pounds, and have a wing span of four feet. The fact that its diet includes rats, gophers, skunks, mice, and even porcupines makes it a vital link in a healthy wildlife community. Fortunately, Wisconsin law protects great horned owls as well as all other owls and hawks. Unfortunately, these tigers of the air also occasionally kill domestic animals such as chickens and turkeys and can become a problem. In most instances a humane trap can be used to capture the troublesome owl. Then it can be released unharmed elsewhere.

Should you ever have a chance to handle a great horned owl BEWARE of its talons. Their grip reminds one of a steel vise. I know of an instance where an unsuspecting and perhaps careless man frightened a great horned owl while handling it and suddenly found the bird's talons deeply buried in his hand. After several painful, unsuccessful attempts to release the talons, the owl's tendons had to be cut in order to free the man.

What sonorous beautiful music flows from the great horned owl. I shall never forget the thrill we got at Wyalusing State Park one perfectly still night as we sat high upon the bluffs overlooking the bayous at the confluence of the Mississippi and Wisconsin rivers. One after another the owls launched into their nighttime songs, which floated up and down the quiet humid river bottoms—music of the gods. What majestic creatures they are, these great horned owls. With their required wild habitat dwindling at a frightening pace, we must do all we can to ensure their survival.

Northwoods Oboist

That stylish, trim, tiny gnome of the northern spruce forest—the red-breasted nuthatch—entertained me royally a few days ago. I have found, from past experience in feeding birds, that, even though this bird sounds like the miniature oboe player of the boreal forest, it plays "second fiddle" to the black-capped chickadee when it comes time to eat.

The suet feeder had been emptied by the birds, and so I decided to fill it. With a fresh supply of food suddenly brought into their frigid "touch and go" winter lives, I expected to see some frenzied activity.

Chickadees, as expected, found it first, and quickly established a regular cafeteria line. Within minutes, two red-breasted nuthatches arrived on the scene and began darting back and forth, from the small jack pine to the hanging feeder. No sooner would they alight on a perch, than they would be unceremoniously chased away with a loud commanding "chik-it" note (meaning SCRAM! in chickadee language).

The longer I watched them, the more I came to feel that the persistent nuthatches were not about to be kept away from the suet. One arrived at the very top of the feeder, landed on the plastic-covered wire, and did a neat half-somersault gripping the wire and hanging headfirst, just able to reach the top suet hole. As long as he remained in this precarious position the chickadees appeared to tolerate their stubby, agile, feathered brother.

Ordinarily I consider red-breasted nuthatches to be lower on the "totem pole" than the chickadees. Frequently, in the past, I have observed chickadees display what appears to be a very impatient, intolerant, condescending attitude toward them. Now, however, the little birds were at the very top!

People seeing these four-inch feathered bundles of perpetual movement for the first time wonder how the word "red" ever came to be a part of the bird's name. One could never, for example, liken its color to

arlotte Lukes

Red-Breasted Nuthatch

that of the red-headed woodpecker. Tawny or rusty would be a more fitting description. Its field marks, however, are easy to see—black cap and eye stripe, blue-gray back, rusty flanks and belly (more so on adult males than on females), and a stubby tail.

Should you be so lucky as to examine the feet of the red-breasted nuthatch, you will probably be surprised at their disproportionately large size. How can you get to see their feet? Easy, if you lure one to food placed in your outstretched hand. To do so, watch closely which feeders they prefer, and allow the birds to empty them. Then put some food in your hand, and stand VERY quiet and motionless next to the empty feeders. Be patient. You will be amazed at how the birds will trust you.

My first success at hand-feeding red-breasted nuthatches occurred on a sub-zero day in January. I had removed my mitten and placed a couple dozen sunflower seeds in my hand; soon the chickadees were dining. Then, suddenly, a bird with a different feel to my fingers landed. It was a red-breasted nuthatch. I marveled at its trusting tameness and the unusual coldness of its feet, but, of course, how could these birds possibly have warm feet when they are repeatedly exposed to below-zero temperatures for several days at a time.

One thing many birders enjoy about this gymnastic ''upside-down'' bird is its day-after-day, week-after-week, never-ending call. Other birds become virtually silent once the nesting season has ended. Not so the red-breasted nuthatch. Its oboe-like call, from my observations, is made without any movement of the mandibles whatsoever, produced entirely in its throat. The call is not at all like the more twangy, nasal, ''ank-ank-ank'' call of the white-breasted nuthatch. It is considerably more mellow and subdued.

The isolated boreal forests of northeastern Wisconsin claim this ''piping red'' as a permanent resident. It is strictly a migratory or winter resident in other parts of the state. Locate a large stand of pines, spruces, or other conifers this winter. There, you will have an excellent chance of seeing one of the most irrepressible, talkative, charming birds of the forest, the red-breasted nuthatch.

Birding On Skis

Ordinarily a person would not expect to encounter signs of spring while cross-country skiing, but that's exactly what happened to a group of us the other day. Air temperature was in the upper teens, and a damp penetrating wind was gusting in from the south, off the bay. The snow was quite crusty in patches, causing us to skitter sideways once in a while. Other than that, however, conditions were just about perfect for skiing.

We stopped frequently to inspect the many shallow animal tracks left in the powdery snow. The meandering trail of a skunk was an unmistakable hint of spring.

Goldeneye ducks and a few buffleheads busied themselves far out on the bay as they dived into the icy water, again and again, in search of food. A large raft of ducks rested and floated just far enough out on the lake so that we had to guess at their identity. Binoculars couldn't pull them in quite close enough. All agreed, however, that they were either lesser or greater scaups. Raft after raft of the ducks will soon be stopping on the shallow coastal bays during their long migratory flight to the north country.

We scooted along the shoreline stopping to survey the lake for more waterfowl. When we spotted a small flock of unidentified ducks, we crouched down for a better look. The thick foliage of the white cedars concealed us from their view, and we identified them as common mergansers—eight of them. Fortunately, they didn't see us as they occupied themselves with their early spring courting ritual.

The flashy males, which outnumbered the females, nervously sliced through the water, changing course frequently. Now and then one would cock his head over his back, then lunge forward with a quick splashy kick of his feet in an effort to impress the apparently unconcerned, aloof females.

We watched them from a distance of about 75 feet, crouching in a low, uncomfortable position, partly concealed by the cedars, until our feet became a bit cold. Then we worked our way down to the snow-covered ice along the shore. Naturally the mergansers took flight the second they saw us and headed across the narrow bay to Fishhead Point. Each performed a beautiful long, running, pattering take-off until all were doing a delicate toe dance on the surface of the water. Seconds later they were airborne.

Close scrutiny of the common merganser (sometimes referred to as the American merganser), indicates that even though it is very duck-like in its appearance and habits, it is also much like the loon. Its feet are situated well back on it body, yet not as far back as the loon's. It walks with difficulty on land, but swims with great power and grace in the water.

I remember an incident a friend and I experienced when we were still in high school. We owned a beat-up old canoe and, judging by the amount of time we spent there, I guess we thought we owned the Kewaunee River, too.

One summer day, we noticed a male common merganser (we called them fish ducks) ahead of us on the river. We decided to see how close we could get to the bird before it took off. To our surprise he didn't fly, but instead, escaped from us by diving under the water and swimming away.

This game of tag continued for a couple of weeks that summer, with us thinking, all the while we were enjoying the sport, that the merganser was injured. Little did we know that his inability to fly resulted from his having lost all of his primary flight feathers, as all adult ducks do just before the young are hatched.

Common mergansers frequently will winter in our county, and a small number will nest in this region, but the majority nest farther north. These two-foot-long beauties are important in the balance of nature because they consume small fish. This is especially important in small northern lakes where the common mergansers help keep the fish population at or below the lakes' full-carrying capacity.

If a lake becomes overpopulated, it will end up having an abundance of small, runty fish. Most fishermen are not interested in catching these particular specimens, but the common mergansers are.

One of my memorable experiences watching a common merganser came early on a summer evening several years ago, as I watched one swim along the mirrorlike surface close to the shoreline of a lake. Every now and then, as it effortlessly skimmed along, its head would probe into the water in search of fish. Suddenly, it would make a quick arched dive forward, nearly clearing the water, and go down after a fish. What a beautiful demonstration of fishing expertise it presented.

Some duck hunters say that the flavor of merganser parallels that of an old kerosene-lantern wick. But one cannot deny the bird's great beauty. It is lovely to behold throughout the year, and it is a special delight when its courtship ritual brings a hint of spring!

The Hawks—Wild And Free

The first thing to greet me early this morning, as I filled the teakettle at the sink and looked out the window, was a female downy woodpecker. She was clinging to a two-inch thick lilac "trunk," her back toward me. The posture did not seem out of the ordinary for I had observed downies in this position dozens of times during the past several years.

As I sat eating breakfast, I noticed that birds were scarce at the north platform feeder. Now and then a chickadee would scoot in for a seed and race back to the spruces to eat it. Frequently, one would buzz in, then wheel about and return to the edge of the thicket without a seed. This behavior was unusual.

I carried the breakfast dishes to the sink to soak—and the downy was right where I had seen her 20 minutes earlier. Now this wasn't quite normal either. There must be a visitor in the yard in search of breakfast, a breakfast that could very well be a downy woodpecker! I scanned as many trees in the yard as I could from the windows. No shrike, no hawk. Whoops! Back up a little—up in the birch behind the garage. There was the threatening force, a fine cooper's hawk. Rusty-barred breast, yellow legs and feet, dark crown, rounded body, including tail, about 18 inches long, scrutinizing every square inch of terrain within a couple hundred feet.

With a little bit of luck perhaps I could get a few pictures of the handsome bird. But the 200 mm. lens just didn't do it justice, so after three pictures I went back into the house for my longest lens. With an adapter attached, my spotting scope grew to the equivalent of about a 1,000 mm. telephoto. This brought the hawk close enough so I could nearly "touch" it. One picture. The bird still sat tight. Closer. Another picture. It began to fidget. Then closer, and that did it. Too close for comfort. Away it flew, down toward the lower light.

What interested me is that all the while I stalked the hawk several goldfinches and chickadees harassed and scolded their natural enemy from only a few feet away, but always keeping above it. Obviously, they knew their limits of safety. And the downy woodpecker, from behind the lilac tree, watched it all—with one eye. The other was hidden, as was nearly all the rest of its body, behind the branch. For fully 15 minutes after the hawk left, the downy never budged. Finally, it inched around to the other side of the branch, head turning, eyes searching the trees in every direction. Now it felt safe to hop onto the suet feeder for some breakfast, perhaps the very thing she was doing when the cooper's hawk arrived looking for its own meal.

One group of hawks, known as accipiters, includes the goshawk, sharp-shinned hawk, and cooper's hawk. The latter two, and possibly all three, nest in Door County. They are characterized by short, rounded wings and long tails. They are slim-bodied and extremely swift of flight, and normally they fly with rapid wing beats and alternate stretches of sailing. Small birds account for nearly all their food.

Unfortunately more than one "bird-watcher" who feeds small songbirds and becomes very fond of them will, in a burst of horrified anger, shoot one of these hawks, because the presence of small birds attracts it to the feeding areas. To many of these bird-watchers the hawk is an evil, vicious creature.

Paul Errington, famous naturalist and writer, said, "It is unfortunate that man, the specialist in evil, sees in predation among wild animals so much evil that isn't there." In my opinion, people who want to feed only certain birds would be better off not feeding any birds at all. Blue jays, red squirrels, hawks, and owls all fall victim to the rifle so that the little songbirds won't be robbed of their food or be chased away.

Fortunately for our hawks and owls, Wisconsin state laws protect all of them. It would be foolhardy to change this law so that only certain species of hawks and owls could be killed, for I contend that in most cases the only persons capable of distinguishing the various species of these birds are those who would not shoot them anyway.

In addition to impressing upon people the vital role these birds of prey play in the balance of nature, more emphasis could be placed upon the very beauty and wildness of these magnificent creatures. Olaus Murie wrote, "A dead eagle is both an economic and a spiritual loss."

Aldo Leopold put it another way: "The swoop of a hawk . . . is perceived by one as the drama of evolution. To another it is only a threat to the full frying pan. The drama may thrill a hundred successive witnesses; the threat only one—for he responds with a shotgun.''

Be patient and alert as you visit many different natural habitats, including swamps, lakeshores, woods, and bogs; eventually some unsuspecting hawk, wild and free as any creature could possibly be, will perform for you a genuine act of nature at its best. Watch and learn, and you'll be a better person for having come to understand, even in some small way, the life of the wild hawk.

Foreign Opportunist

A regretful, perhaps unforgivable event took place in New York City's Central Park back before the turn of the century, which, for all I know, is today making residents of Graceham, Maryland clench their fists in anger and disgust.

It was in 1890 that 80 European starlings (*Sturnus vulgaris*) were released into a new environment, the North American continent. Little did Eugene Scheifflin, who engineered the plan, realize the seriousness of that act. Quite innocently he and his band of followers were attempting to introduce to the United States all of the plants and animals mentioned in the works of Shakespeare.

But recently, a 60-acre wooded area near Graceham was inundated by upwards of 10 million starlings, grackles, and blackbirds. I suspect that the tough, wiry starlings make up the majority of this damaging, nerve-wracking, and even health-threatening flock.

Many people are able to recognize this wheezy-voiced foreigner of questionable value. It has been described as a black songbird, about the size of a robin, having a long pointed beak, short swept-back wings, and a stubby tail. Its straight, direct flight is much like that of its cousin, the meadowlark, as it flaps its wings several times, then glides for a short distance; flaps, glides; flaps, glides.

The starling I examined "in the hand" last fall amazed me with the dazzling beauty of its winter plumage. Having just completed its single molt of the year, the bird was sporting new wing feathers that were edged with a light buffy tan. Other smaller body feathers appeared to be tipped with a soft yellowish tan. The colored areas, or "star spots," on the feather-tips form small V-shapes, giving the bird a speckled appearance from a distance, and accounting for the bird's name—starling means "little star." Gradually, during the winter and spring, the light feather edges wear off; by spring, the bird is a shiny, glossy black, laced with exciting irridescent shades of bronze, blue, green, and lilac.

Because of its strong legs and feet, the starling gives the appearance of being the proud possessor of a quick, nervous, cocky waddle. It doesn't hop, as do most other songbirds. That's right. It is a songbird, and an excellent mimic at that! Its wheezy, grating, raspy whistles have confused many people, especially when it quite expertly imitates other bird calls. However, it does not rank with the mockingbird in expertise.

This omnivorous opportunist is considered by many to be of great value in the balance of nature because of its voracious appetite for injurious animals, including land snails, cutworms, and Japanese beetles. My friend Elmer DeCramer, wise in the ways of many birds, heard me complain about starlings one day and sided with the black bandits. He advised me to watch a starling closely the next time I saw one strutting around the lawn. When I did so, I noticed that the bird would drive its closed spearlike beak straight down into the grass, then open it up, spreading apart the blades of grass as it searched for insects. In this industrious manner the methodical little hunter consumed one insect after another.

A study has shown that the diet of midwestern starlings is composed of about 57 percent animal and 43 percent vegetable material. Many starlings I have watched arriving at their nest holes had their beaks virtually dripping with fat, wriggling, green caterpillars. Frequently, one can see these wily birds feeding on the ground in the vicinity of cattle, capturing the insects stirred up by the feet of the livestock.

It is during fruit-ripening time that starlings become serious pests. They can virtually destroy an entire cherry, apple, or pear orchard, or a vineyard. Their autumn appetite for fruit is legendary and is known in most countries of the world, including New Zealand where they were introduced by Europeans in 1862. Starlings, along with their partners in crime, the house sparrows, are very likely the most common birds in the world today.

Starlings associate with man amazingly well. As various forms of agriculture succeed, so do starlings. Those noisy nuisances reached Wisconsin in about 1923, and within about 30 years they had become securely established over the entire west coast of America. Their abundance is compounded by the fact that starlings have been known to live to be 18 years old!

Most starlings in this region are migratory, even though a small number of them are observed on winter bird censuses each year. By the way, they are not protected by Wisconsin law. Paired adults very likely have at least two, and sometimes three, broods annually. The immature birds are brownish-gray; they gather into sizable early summer flocks. Occasionally, you will see one or a small number of black unattached adults flying with a young, inexperienced group. Several years ago, we were lucky to spot an albino starling in one of these "synchronized-moving" flocks, as it drifted across the grain-stubble fields in search of food.

About 107 distinct species of starlings can be found throughout the world. Several, such as the hill myna of India, are expert "talkers." Others, including the golden-crested starling, the superb starling of East Africa, the rosy pastor of Southeastern Europe, and the amethyst starling of Tropical Africa, are almost unbelievable in the beauty of their colors.

If you've never seen the starlings' intricate evening aerial maneuvers en masse as they return to roost, you're in for a pleasant surprise. This mysterious wide-sweeping social dance, sometimes staged by several million at a time, is thought to help keep the flock together.

Supposing that native songbirds of this country could talk, many of the hole-nesters would be bitterly opposed to the fierce, aggressive takeover tactics of the starlings. Wrens, bluebirds, nuthatches, tree swallows, woodpeckers, crested flycatchers, and purple martins have all suffered the encroachment of these foreigners.

Whether or not you appreciate the starling is a matter for individual decision. But the more one observes and learns about this nest robber, garbage eater, musical mimic, destroyer of harmful insects, and connoisseur of fruit, the more one thinks of the starling as the Jekyll-and-Hyde of the bird world.

Keeper Of The Marsh

I encounter the first day of spring with mixed feelings, while at least a foot and a half of snow still blankets the ground. Inevitably, I think about the early arriving birds, and I find myself ascribing human reactions to them. I wonder if they are reconsidering the wisdom of having embarked on their northward journey so early. As an example of their predicament, six killdeers nervously tiptoed up and down the shoulder of the highway yesterday morning, looking for something to eat. Meadowlarks and horned larks, too, have been tightly confined to the roadsides in their painstaking search for food.

But the real out-of-place spring welcome came yesterday as Earl Swenson and I were returning, on snowshoes, from a jaunt out to Toft's Point and along Moonlight Bay. We had been setting a brisk pace and were looking forward to reaching our car, parked out along the road. Suddenly I stopped in my tracks and asked, ''Was that a red-winged blackbird that just sang?'' We waited a minute and soon the redwing answered my question. ''O-ka-leee, O-ka-leee.'' Nothing—no nothing—comes even close to making the delightful musical call of this dapper creature of the wetlands and fields.

To many people this is the first real song of spring. How beautifully it carries. ''O-ka-lee, O-ka-la-ree, ong-ka-lee, conk-kar-eee.'' These are a few of the phonetic analyses people have associated with the male redwing's song. As more and more redwings are joined by song sparrows and other equally good singers, the beauty of their song tends to wear off. But the sound of that very first call thrills me right down to my toes. Perhaps it is its reassurance of spring's arrival that makes the call most welcome, for redwings don't make seasonal mistakes.

Few people realize the importance of the songs of birds, but fewer know that redwing blackbirds combine their songs with a marvelous display of colors. Call it a song-spread display.

Observe a male redwing sing and you will note that his head is thrust forward, tail and wings are lowered, and his red shoulder patches, his epaulets of authority, tend to enlarge and puff up. When the bird produces the ''LEE'' portion of his song, his posture has reached its extreme contortion. Now he means business. Every ounce of his body seems to be thrown into a shrill, colorful challenge to all other male redwings within sight or hearing.

The crux of the matter is that in order to get a mate, the male must have a territory, and territories don't just happen to come about without a fight. In order to announce his presence to the world, the male redwing perches on the highest stalk or branch in his territory—which ranges from about 1,000 to about 10,000 square feet—and pours forth his musical challenge. If you should get too close to his home ground, or, in particular, to one of his mate's nests, you are in for a rude reception—a rather sharp ''chuck-chuck-chuck'' and the possibility of a threatened pass at your head!

Recently, an ornithologist trying to learn more about the song-spread display of the male redwing captured a number of them and dyed their bright crimson epaulets black. Some of the altered males lost their territories after they had been stripped of their colors, but others seemed to be unaffected. As a matter of fact, some lured as many as six females into their territories. (Yes, redwings are polygamous!) The conclusion of this study was that females choose a male on the basis of his territory, not on the flash and color of his epaulets, nor on the beauty of his singing. His epaulets do serve, however, to challenge and to intimidate other males.

I shall always remember a redwing experience I had several years ago, while observing whistling swans at Mud Lake, north of Madison. I had hidden myself in the tall grass in back of a fence on a small knoll overlooking the edge of the marshy lake. The swans gradually moved in until they were only about 50 yards away, where they gabbled and fed quite peacefully. It was all my show, or at least so I thought, until a brilliant male redwing flew to the top of a stubby post between me and the swans, perhaps 20 yards away. This proved to be the high point of his territory, his singing perch. Over and over he laced out with his ''O-ka-lee'' melody, sometimes facing directly toward me, his red shoulder patches blazing in the late afternoon sun. Here was the real star of the show. He wasn't about to let the swans steal the spotlight from him. And they didn't.

To this day the singing star of my spring stage continues to be the male red-winged blackbird. Polygamous, aggressive, at times unknowingly destructive of farmers' crops—none of these traits will prevent this flashy master of the marshes from being the champion songster of early spring. Mr. Redwing, welcome back!

Bobbing Butterballs

A cold stinging rain from out of the south is causing the tag alders, hanging heavy with dripping deep-red catkins, to sway enough so that the evening grosbeaks and pine siskins have to balance and bob precariously as they wait their turns at the feeders. In one sense the rain is welcome. At least it is not snow, such as we had last week. Instead, the unwelcome and unseasonable ''white stuff'' is fast disappearing this morning.

Some folks would say this weather isn't even fit for ducks. However, if one were to analyze the existing bay and lake conditions, pelting rain included, from the ducks' viewpoint, both rain and stormy lake surface would be welcome. The shallow bay area, rich in natural food and ideally suited for the diving waterfowl, now belongs to them—as it should! These diving ducks, including the redhead, canvasback, ring-necked, scaup, and bufflehead are now at peace in their world.

Put several dozen chugging, trolling motorboats carrying sport fishermen on every bay along the coast and you displace most of the ducks. They take off in search of the next best feeding areas. Where these areas are I don't know. In one sense I believe our native waterfowl are suffering at the expense of the thousands upon thousands of trout and salmon planted in Lake Michigan, which in turn are bringing about a sport fishing craze that has never been seen here before. Little or no interest, to my knowledge, has been exhibited in support of the ducks' problem.

The ducks have no spokesman, and yet their actions speak with clarity and appeal to anyone who will take the time to observe their numbers and feeding habits over a period of years. It's another glaring example of the adverse impact of our growing, expanding society upon the native animals. The monetary and political ''wallop'' of our present-day industrialists, developers, and leaders is staggering, and the majority of the people don't really seem to care. If only the ducks and other native animals could have lobbying powers with which to challenge our leaders' decisions, our ''Great Outdoors'' wouldn't be in its present deplorable condition.

One of the ducks that bob corklike on the choppy waters of the bay today is also one of the smallest to stop over here, the bufflehead. Some call it buffalo-head, a name that dates back to olden days when the head of this short-necked stocky duck was likened to the general shape of a buffalo's head. Butterball and spirit duck describe this dashing water bird very well, too. Watch a small group of them in the early spring and you will soon agree that they are active and spirited, always on the move.

Because the drake buffleheads have such bold black and white markings, including a large white head patch, they could be described as graceful white ducks. Their scientific name, *Charitonetta albeola*, says exactly this. *Charitos*, in Greek, means grace, and *netta* means duck. *Albeola*, in Latin, refers to white. The female has much less white, but the white spot on the side of her head in back of her eye is an important field mark.

To see the drakes from close range in sunlight, their heads flashing a deep irridescent purple and green color, is a rare treat. About the only duck with which it might be confused is the hooded merganser.

Hunters who shoot buffleheads and attempt to eat them are most often disappointed, perhaps even shocked. Any duck that feeds largely upon small fish and other aquatic animal life will have an undesirable flavor. We attempted to eat an old squaw duck one time and were nearly driven out of the house by the odor of the animal as it cooked. Most buffleheads will be found to be much the same.

There are few ducks I enjoy watching more in the spring of the year than the bufflehead. Only 14 to 15 inches in length, it appears to ride the water very buoyantly. What a graceful diver it is! Take your eyes off this creature for a second and it will have disappeared. It can remain under water for as long as 20 seconds. And should one of them come up to the surface with danger apparent, it will take to the air almost as though it had begun flying while under water. Talk about a speedy takeoff! Most diving ducks tend to have a splashy running-on-the-water takeoff.

The bufflehead comes in for a landing about as abruptly as it takes off, with a hard splash. Its flight tends to be quite low over the water.

Like wood ducks and goldeneyes, the bufflehead is also a hole-nesting bird. Frequently, buffleheads use abandoned woodpecker cavities; for instance, that of the flicker. They are known to squeeze in and out of a hole as small as three inches or slightly larger. Their primary summer breeding grounds are to the north and west of the prairies of Canada.

Even though it was raining today as we observed the antics of the buffleheads, they seemed to be carrying on quite normally. All were busy diving for food and oiling their feathers as they bobbed about on the choppy bay. They reached around repeatedly to oil glands above their tails, then quickly brushed their oily beaks through their feathers. Between periods of feeding and preening, the males were courting the females. They appeared determined to attract as many females as they could. In one group two males were challenging each other over five females. The males would pump their heads up and down about seven or eight times as they swam in tight little arcs and circles.

Include the buffleheads in your spring observations. Better yet, record your observations on paper from year to year. Accurate amateur observations over a period of many years may contribute to the preservation of these animals. I would hate to see a spring arrive without buffleheads using the bay for feeding and resting. For the very spirit of spring is wrapped up within these bobbing little bundles of black and white feathers.

Buffalobirds

This morning, a male yellow-bellied sapsucker clung tightly to the upper trunk of a horse chestnut tree in the lee of the pelting rain and called out every 15 seconds or so with his sharp "peer-peer" notes. If these calls voiced his displeasure with the weather, I wonder what he was saying yesterday during our Easter snowstorm!

Anyone who has lived for several years in east-central Wisconsin will have come to expect these unwelcome blasts of cold, damp Lake Michigan air. Happily, this unpleasantness usually is accompanied by the return of large flocks of juncos passing through, the first flashy fox sparrow of the season, and, now and then, a winter wren, myrtle warbler, Brewer's blackbird, or cowbird.

As often happens, when we saw our first cowbird of the season on Easter morning, we had to take a second look before we were sure of who this mousy-gray newcomer was that had joined the other birds at the feeders. After studying its color and rather stout bill, it dawned on us: Nothing but a shiftless tramp of a female brown-headed cowbird.

Many bird enthusiasts despise the parasitic nesting habits of this "brownhead." And, indeed, its Latin name, *Molothrus ater*, refers to a dark, greedy beggar. However, if you take a closer look at this carefree villain, perhaps you'll develop a slightly different outlook toward it.

I saw my first large flocks of cowbirds at the beginning of my serious bird-watching career while in the Army at Fort Sill, Oklahoma. I frequently observed hundreds of them following large herds of buffalo that inhabited the wide-open prairies on the post. The buffalo, as they ambled through the grass, roused numerous insects into movement; and the insects, in turn, promptly were eaten by the cowbirds (buffalobirds!).

Later, during my studies, I wondered whether it was this habit of following buffalo and cattle that led cowbirds to lay their eggs in other birds' nests. Could it be possible that with the birds having to range so far from their nest sites when accompanying the cattle, it is absolutely *essential* that they lay their eggs somewhere where they will be taken care of? Unfortunately there are few, if any, facts supporting such an idea, so this suggestion remains a mere guess.

Strangely, these monogamous birds set up a rather well-defined territory. The black, irridescent, brown-headed male first establishes his summer quarters, and then awaits the arrival of the female, whom he attracts with a humorous, wheezy, frenzied display. While other birds prepare for nesting, these two proceed to search for weed seeds and insects. Then begins the villainous act so many people detest. The female, moving in a manner that some observers have described as being sly and stealthy, locates another bird's nest and lay's a single egg in it.

Studies have shown that the single egg the cowbird lays will most often hatch before the host bird's eggs. As a result, the young cowbird receives the majority, if not all, of the food brought to the nest by the mother bird. Thus, one sometimes observes what appears to be the puzzling phenomenon of a small songbird feeding an oversized noisy, begging baby—the young cowbird.

At least 206 species of birds are known to be victimized by the cowbird. Warblers, vireos, various types of sparrows—but especially song and chipping sparrows—appear to head the list of unfortunate hosts. Additional study is needed in order to determine the percentage of ''good'' birds that will re-nest in a more hidden and favorable site after having been victimized by the cowbird. And this suggests another hypothesis: Could it be possible that the majority of parasitized nests are those of birds nesting for the first time? Perhaps this experience makes them better nest builders the second time.

One should study all of the available facts before completely condemning a particular bird species. Clearly, the brown-headed cowbird does a tremendous amount of good by eating great numbers of harmful insects. We are, then, forced to admit that these feathered vagabonds are neither bad nor good. In fact, if we would carefully examine the total web of animal life, each species in its own niche, we would be surprised to find that, by our standards, *many* birds are not as harmless or beneficial as we might have thought they were. And yet, each species appears to be of special value to its environment in one way or another.

By the way, here is an interesting exercise for you. Try listing the reasons you feel you are an asset or a detriment to *your* environment. I have an idea that your list of the ways you add to the deterioration of the environment could very well be longer than your list of positive contributions. At least mine works out that way! Perhaps this will help you see why I am sympathetic to that brown-headed ''hanger-on,'' the cowbird.

Prairie Hoedown

The last-quarter moon produced beautiful reflections on the lake, backlighting the Lower Rangelight this morning at 4 A.M. Only one bird made its presence known in the back meadow at this early moonlit hour, the woodcock. He, too, would have foregone his peenting, were it not for the clear skies and the waning moon.

I sit here in the quiet study recalling a particular March weekend in 1956. Ray White, of Madison, where I was teaching then, invited me to spend the weekend helping Drs. Fred and Fran Hamerstrom with their prairie chicken project on the Buena Vista marsh southeast of Wisconsin Rapids. It was one of those experiences that now, 20 years later, I consider a turning point in my life.

For the most part, the weekend was filled with work. I certainly hadn't visualized using a needle and thread, or hammer and nails, when Ray invited me to come along to "look for prairie chickens," but wooden and canvas blinds needed repairs. And when the repairing was completed, we donned hipboots, sloshed through wet ditches carrying the blinds on our shoulders, and staked them in place under the careful eyes of Fred and Fran.

Our first glimpse of the prairie chickens occurred as we helped with what is called "flush counts." First we glassed the stubble fields where the birds were known to be. Then, stalking slowly and carefully, we approached them until suddenly, with a flurry of wings, off they flew. Each of us took as accurate a count as we could, then compared our figures for the final tally.

Last Saturday, 20 years and one month later, my wife and I spent four hours crouched in a blind studying and photographing the "prairie boomers." We had reserved this blind a year in advance, and, after a year of waiting, we awoke to a 2:30 A.M. alarm to find a driving rainstorm! What a letdown.

Ours was one of four cars that met the DNR representative at precisely 3:15 in the morning, and followed him down narrow dirt roads laced with ruts and puddles. One by one, each group was assigned to its study area. Almost unbelieving, we stopped near our appointed destination. Our man aimed a powerful beam of light into the darkness and said, "Walk that plank over the drainage ditch. It'll hold you. Crawl under the barbed wire fence and continue walking in the direction I'm shining the light. Eventually you should come to the blind. Get in quickly, sit down, and be quiet."

What a sorry sight we must have presented to the prairie chickens somewhere out there in the darkness. But we found the blind and were glad to get out of the driving rain. Fortunately, it soon stopped and our spirits turned upward. Songs of the western meadowlark, song sparrow, horned lark, Wilson's snipe, and woodcock assured us that daylight was just around the corner.

The first cock prairie chicken flew into the area at 4:15 A.M. and immediately began his booming. Charlotte looked out of one of the tiny observation holes expecting the bird to be within a few feet of the blind but found it to be about 50 feet away. The rain "piddled" on and off as a total of eight cocks arrived at their booming grounds. Here they would defend their territories for the next four hours, producing their unbelievably interesting and beautiful love calls, trying desperately to attract one or more hens to the "most beautiful and handsome male prairie chicken in the world."

Say the words, "you ole fool, you ole fool," over and over, pronouncing the word "you" at a normal speed, but extending the world "ole" and "fool" with long o's and rolling l's. This will give you an idea of the booming sounds, and will also tell you what we felt like, crawling on our hands and knees under a barbed wire fence at 3:45 A.M. in a pelting rainstorm!

We soon forgot our cold, damp misery as the light of dawn illuminated the magnificent wild birds. Short runs and abrupt stops, quick pattering stamps of their feet upon the ground, inflating of brilliant orange sacs on the sides of the neck, head thrust downward, neck tufts held upward, tail raised and spread—all these actions characterized their "dancing."

Six sandhill cranes, bugling as they flew with necks outstretched, passed to the front of the blind, adding to the excitement. One turned back as though parading in review, giving us a special treat and cheering us up in our wet, cramped quarters.

Four hours passed quickly as we recorded on paper everything we could observe about the prairie chickens: which ones were banded, the numbers on the bands, the limits of individuals' territories, etc. Finally, the eight birds left for their feeding areas, and we headed for some hot coffee, happy through and through that we had helped the experts in a tiny way to learn more about the habits of the few remaining "prairie boomers." We concluded, unquestionably, that these wild creatures of the cool April prairies had given us their message: "We need your help. Preserve our habitat!"

All-American Bird

There are few things my wife and I look forward to more each year than keeping a chronological list of birds as they arrive at the Sanctuary in spring. One of our favorites was heard singing somewhere back in the tag alders on March 20. Few sportsmen who hunt game during the season would be able to tell you which game animal ranks first in numbers shot annually by hunters in the United States. The answer is this early spring visitor—the mourning dove! Yet, Wisconsin and about 20 other states consider it a songbird and protect it throughout the year!

Imagine how surprised I was—while listening to a lecture presented by a wildlife biologist pertaining to the trapping of mourning doves—to learn that as many as 40 million are shot each year. Compare this to approximately 14 million waterfowl, including ducks and geese, gunned down yearly during hunting season.

If you would have told me as a boy (during summer vacations, when I was cutting the lawn at John Proctor's in Kewaunee) that the birds cooing so dolefuly, high in the backyard elm trees, might be shot by hunters in Illinois or other states to the south of us that fall—well, I just wouldn't have believed you.

As sad and mournful as their calls were, I really looked forward to hearing them. The peaceful, shady expansiveness of those yards would have been incomplete without the mourning dove music.

Chances are pretty good that the doves we saw and heard here a couple of weeks ago are the same ones that wintered nearby. Even though they are migratory birds, the same phenomenon occurs with them as with many other species. Those that nest farthest north, say southern Canada, will not migrate as far south as those that nest in Door County.

Even though the names pigeon and dove are used interchangeably, they do have individual characteristics that set them apart. Pigeons tend to be larger and chunkier, and to have square or rounded tails.

Doves are smaller and more graceful, and have longer pointed tails. More than 280 species of doves inhabit various countries of the world.

The sleek, streamlined appearance of the foot-long mourning dove is enhanced by its pinkish-gray color and the subtle bronzy, pink-and-violet coloring of the top and sides of its neck. The prominent white tips of its tail feathers are accentuated when the bird is in flight and its tail is fanned into a long V-shaped wedge outlined in white.

Its swift powerful flight makes it appear to weigh more than its actual four ounces. The first mourning dove I handled taught me a thing or two about its power. Friends of mine northwest of Green Bay were feeding more than 70 of them every morning one early spring, along with dozens of purple finches and evening grosbeaks, and several of each species were captured in my banding nets.

What a powerful handful of bird I had when I removed the first dove. Surprisingly, a couple of the birds I examined were missing all or most of their toes on both feet, yet appeared to be in good health. Perhaps the most accurate guess would be that they were victims of a type of foot disease, one of several quite common to birds.

The more I think of it, the more I feel that the mourning dove would have been the perfect choice to be our national bird because it nests in every state except Hawaii. Its distribution and abundance are also attested to by the fact that this gray ghost of the fields is legal game in 30 states, mostly in the south and west.

How well I remember my boyhood days and the dove nests built in the Norway spruces in our yard! Often I wondered why their nests were so flimsy. Now, when I examine their feet and beaks, it becomes obvious that the birds are simply incapable of building better nests. Records show that rains and storms of 1973 were so frequent that many dove eggs and nests were destroyed. Unfortunately there was not enough time between storms for the birds to re-nest and, consequently, the mourning doves suffered a noticeable decline in numbers that year.

This gentle elusive bird, known for its whistling flight, has responded quite favorably to changes brought about by man. Tree plantings by settlers on the open prairies gave the doves good nesting sites. Watering holes that were created for cattle answered the same need for these birds. Overgrazing and poor land management, both favoring the growth of weeds, helped provide the mourning doves with plenty of food. Modern-day harvesting methods, including the use of combines and cornpickers, leave a considerable amount of food in the fields easily found by these keen-eyed strong flyers.

We fervently hope the day never dawns when the last bald eagle will have made its final soaring flight into the realm of extinction. Just in case, though, to be on the safe side, what do you think about the idea of choosing the all-American bird? My vote? Without a doubt—the mourning dove!

Black Marauders

Picture a handsome black bird about a foot long, with glossy iridescent shades of bronze, violet, green, and purple on its head and upper body. Add to that a dignified, swaggering walk and you have visualized that very bold bird, the grackle.

Like the robins, starlings, waterfowl, and red-winged blackbirds, grackles migrate during daylight hours in the footsteps of spring. They remind me of adventurous (sometimes naughty) little boys who enjoy mud puddles, small rivulets, and getting as close to water—or into its shallow parts—without getting too wet. In this respect I, too, would have been a typical grackle.

Several distinct races of grackles have been identified including the purple, Florida, and bronzed. Apparently the degree of crossbreeding has been such that, for this region, the races have become indistinguishable. Alas, this sleek bird with the long shoehorn-like tail has been tabbed the common grackle. But I suppose any bird whose range extends from southern Canada south into Alabama and Georgia is, indeed, common.

Mention these audacious black marauders to some people and you're in for an argument. Unprintable words might flow. Perhaps it is the grackles' racket—call it their squeaky wheelbarrow chorus—that raises the dander of some folks. And, too, the heinous label of nest-robber has been associated with the grackle for years; this hasn't improved the bird's image.

If one were to examine the food habits of these resourceful animals, one would find both creditable and discreditable behavior. Grubs, weed seeds, and especially grasshoppers are included in their diets. In fact, their young are fed mostly insects. But farmers point an accusing finger at these greedy birds when they inspect corn and grain damage. Yet research has shown that the grackles' maximum consumption of corn occurs during February so this could only be waste corn lying on the ground.

The pompous musical "performance" of the males is amusing to some, annoying to others. Watch a flashy male in his breeding plumage puff up his chest as though he were being inflated in readiness for a grandiose vocal performance. Instead, out struggles the squeakiest, raspiest, rustiest, "chacking" call you could imagine. Mr. A. A. Saunders, a bird-song expert, has described the grackle's song as saying, "Kuchaku-wee-ee-K-ee-Ku-waa-a!"

Should you have evergreen trees, such as spruces, on your property you stand a good chance of having grackles nest there—not only one pair, but several. These birds are quite communal in their nesting habits. Their wide tolerance for nesting sites and food reflects their high degree of adaptiveness. Undoubtedly their numbers are on the increase.

Many people have asked, "Can we shoot grackles?" Wisconsin law protects common grackles. But to confuse the issue, Part 16, Title 50 of the Code of Federal Regulations indicates that a person may destroy blackbirds, cowbirds, and grackles without a permit when they are committing serious depredations, or are about to do so, to ornamental and shade trees and agricultural crops.

Birds not protected by Wisconsin law include red-winged blackbirds, cowbirds, starlings, house sparrows, and crows (during certain seasons). Some experts seriously believe that common grackles should be added to this list. One thing is certain. It would be well for state and federal wildlife agencies to reach agreement on laws pertaining to protecting or not protecting certain species.

Wholesale slaughter, regardless of the method, has proven to be unpopular—and to many, unethical. Obviously there is no kind way of destroying millions of birds. Perhaps an effective means of biological control can be found. Certainly good management must be considered. More emphasis must be placed upon the question, "What can WE do to help the situation?"

Adding another bird to the list of those that can legally be shot would compound the already existing problem of scores of songbirds being shot, regardless of species. One wildlife biologist recommended that any person purchasing a hunting license should have to pass a species identification test. Gun safety, taught in schools or by sportsmen's clubs, should also emphasize accurate identification of all species that can be shot legally.

You ask what my opinion on the matter is? My answer is,

"Kuchakee-wee-ee-K-ee-Ku-waa-a!" Or, in people language, "Wouldn't it be nice if the grackles had a voice in the great decision for others to take their lives?"

King Of The Waterfowl

The king of all waterfowl has been causing me to take a ''longcut'' home from school each day during the past week. All of you know what a shortcut is. I first learned what a longcut was when I was in kindergarten. It's simply a much longer than usual route between school and home. It always occurs on the way home.

Joe Lichterman, who was a Kewaunee mailman when I was a youngster, was the cause of my first delayed, roundabout routes home at noon. We usually tagged onto him where the Allens used to live, across from the Congregational church. It was great sport to ''help'' him deliver the mail. That fun lasted until I kept lunch waiting once too often and received a good seat warming from my dad.

The king that has been bringing about my recent longcuts is the whistling swan. For even though the flooded fields have resulted in misery for some area farmers, the waterfowl attracted to these temporary bodies of water are bringing unexpected joy to dozens of people fortunate enough to observe them.

One nice thing about the arrival of 145 swans is that they are sure evidence of the onset of spring. For centuries, the swans have been following various routes, including this one along western Lake Michigan, to their breeding grounds.

Their total migratory route from the Maryland coast, then to northeastern Wisconsin, and finally up to the low Arctic region lying north of the Hudson Bay and the Arctic Circle shows that they incorporate a considerable dogleg into their long journey. Generally they make the trip with only one major rest stop. Considering the fact that these powerful birds, with a wingspan of seven feet, cruise at about 50 m.p.h., the last leg of their migratory flight will take them approximately 30 hours.

I'd give anything to be able to live for one year as a swan. So help me, someday I'm going to trace the route of the swan, even though it will be on the ground, just to satisfy a strange desire deep inside of me.

I know that one can take a train up to the southwestern coast of the Hudson Bay, the southernmost limit of the whistlers' summer environment, and that would be good enough for me. The earlier part of the route would be easy to follow by automobile.

I'm not so sure I'd arrive at their breeding grounds when they do, in early May. The soft, slushy snow that remains makes foot-travel by humans next to impossible and is one of the major factors ensuring successful predator-free nesting.

A barren environment, far away from humans, has for centuries been a necessity in the lives of these early nesters. It is difficult to imagine a nest more conspicuous than that of the swan. Picture a large white bird sitting on top of a muskrat house in the middle of a square mile of flat, marshy expanse. Little wonder that they require seclusion.

The young are ready to leave the nest by early July, but until that point is reached, nature has provided them with very dependable babysitters. For adults lose all their primary wing feathers during nesting and thus are absolutely flightless. This forces them to remain with the cygnets.

The new birds will be flying by the middle of September, having been fattened by eating plants such as wild celery, grass, pondweed, and smartweed. Their southerly flight, which may include stretches flown at altitudes as high as 8,000 feet (proven by swan-plane collisions), will begin by mid-October. Five months up north, seven months down south—quite similar to human ''snowbirds''!

How I enjoyed watching the swans dabble for submerged stalks of corn. Someone asked me, ''How far down into the water can a swan reach for food?'' Their total length is about 52 inches, and only about one foot of their tail end shows above the surface as they search for underwater morsels. That gives them a reach of more than a yard.

Last Friday, my longcut home required more time than usual. Not only were the swans noticeably talkative and alert, but their duck companions also were putting on a lively performance—blue-winged teal, scaup, widgeon, goldeneye, green-winged teal, pintail, mallard, canvasback, redhead, and ring-necked. One could sense excitement in the wind as the stately, straight-necked swans displayed considerably more head pumping and wing fanning than usual.

Saturday morning told the story. The swans were gone. Something had prompted their move to another resting and feeding spot between here and the Arctic. Where? I wish I knew. I rejoice over their brief but spectacular show and will gladly wait for next spring and some more longcuts to see the king of all waterfowl, the whistling swan.

Dancers In The Duff

A handsome little band of pugnacious, transient fox sparrows arrived here the day before the spring election, during the worst blizzard of the winter. Some of our friends had already raked their lawns and were on the verge of tilling their gardens when the snow began. We suspect that a number of the colorful and robust sparrows had been around since the last days of March, and that it was the severe storm that caused them to concentrate near our feeders.

Past records tell us to begin looking for fox sparrows when patches of snow still linger in the area. In fact, the little birds are known to arrive here so early, often in company with juncos and tree sparrows, that it is highly probable they will encounter at least one bad snow or ice storm before reaching their summer breeding territory far to the north.

I wish this bird might have received a name other than sparrow. Unfortunately, too many people, upon hearing a name other than sparrow, associate the creature with the lowly house sparrow. But fox sparrows are strictly first-class birds. The brilliant cinnamon color of their tails and wings accentuates the activeness of these ''dancers in the duff.'' And their habit of scratching for food with vigorous backward hops, both feet in motion at the same time, is a reliable sign to look for, much like that of the towhee.

The April 4 blizzard that dropped 13½ inches of heavy wet snow here tended to tighten the little groups of migratory birds. Charlotte attempted to keep one step ahead of the storm by periodically sweeping the snow off the feeders and the ground beneath them. The birds responded beautifully. By the next morning, 10 of these shy beauties, the fox sparrows, were seen together, all busily excavating shallow little depressions in the snow and sunflower seed hulls in search of food. It has been determined that small groups of up to a dozen are likely to remain together during the entire migration.

Although most of these boldly marked birds are known as migrants, there are exceptions. Several much darker races nest in some of the northwestern states. The fox sparrows we encounter for about a two-week period each spring belong to 1 of approximately 18 subspecies. Only the song sparrow and horned lark are known to have more subspecies. Chances are good that these present visitors will nest as far north as the Hudson Bay coast.

With the fox sparrows so close to the north kitchen windows, it was an easy matter to observe them from every angle. Ruddy, rusty, or rich chestnut describes their most noticeable color. The throat, chest, and belly are white and heavily streaked with arrow marks of dark brown. In addition, the throat is bordered with bold rusty triangular-shaped patches that are more outstanding than the breast streaks. Most of the birds tend to have a larger dark spot in the upper middle of the breast. The lower mandible is a flesh to light yellow color. The legs and feet are pink.

Whenever an unusually loud car or truck goes by, or when I step outside on my way to the woodshed, the fox sparrows are the first of the birds to vanish. I've watched them closely and have learned that most usually they fly upward about 8 or 10 feet to conceal themselves among the thick branches of the white spruces. There they remain motionless watching cautiously until the "danger" has passed. Juncos will dribble slowly back to the feeding area first. Then, when the coast is absolutely clear, the fox sparrows return to resume their scratching. Not only do they bear the coloring of a fox, but they seem to have developed some of his shyness, as well!

During their migration, these sturdily built little excavators feed primarily on seeds. Small wild fruits and ragweed and smartweed seeds constitute much of their food. Seldom have I seen them chase another bird species, such as a junco, away from their feeding area. However, if another fox sparrow gets too near, a brief spat is likely to arise between the two. As close-knit as the group may be during migration, they demand plenty of elbow room when it comes time to search for food.

The balmy but brisk southerly wind, carrying record-breaking warmth, today has plugged our harbor full of drift ice. For the songbirds, the need to be wary of the constant movement of the trees is heightened by the presence of several sharp-shinned hawks. Yet the songs of the juncos and fox sparrows flavor the warm breeze liberally despite the ever-present alert signals.

How longingly we wait for the fox sparrows' arrival each spring. Many mornings we wake up early just to watch them, not wanting to miss a single performance of their "dancing in the duff at dawn's early light." One of these springs, we are not going to be content with their two-week visit, but instead will pack our camping gear and head north with them to their nesting grounds near the shores of Hudson Bay, or even eastward into Newfoundland. It is there that these strong singers, with the clear brilliant songs bursting with joy, reveal what they are like at their best. Their "teasing" two-week visit, serves only to whet our appetites for more.

The Bird With A Sweet Tooth

Two pleasant surprises greeted me early this morning as I took my customary glance out the east kitchen window. Two large deer, both does, grazed contentedly out in the back meadow, and a yellow-bellied sapsucker, sharply silhouetted by the morning backlighting, clung to the north side of one of the large sugar maple tree trunks, seemingly spellbound, glued to the spot, lapping up his breakfast of maple sap.

Each day, the deer appear increasingly to be coming out of their winter jitters, and are ranging closer to the house. In the morning I can tell how near they have been by examining their tracks in the slushy ice that remains on the front concrete walk.

The male sapsuckers have been here for about a week. Their brilliant scarlet-colored foreheads and chins clearly help one to distinguish them from the females. The females' foreheads are scarlet, too, but their chins are white. Surrounding woods resound with sapsucker chatter and scolding once the females arrive on the scene. Males telegraph their locations for the whole world to hear, or so you would think. But it is for the females that they send out their locating calls. They have that wonderful knack of choosing just the right tree branch which, when beaten against with their beaks, resounds with great percussive beauty for several hundred yards.

Woe to the male that invades another male sapsucker's proclaimed territory, especially if the first inhabitant has already succeeded in attracting a female. If this occurs in your presence, you're in for a show. What excitement! What activity as the males go after one another—hiding, peeking, chasing, scolding, fighting, not letting up for one second. Should you be in an area where maple trees grow near a quiet bay, stream, or pond, be on the lookout for this marvelous display. This is the general type of area that yellow-bellied sapsuckers tend to prefer.

If you were to examine a sapsucker's tongue, you would be amazed to discover that it is quite brushlike and not nearly as long, spiny, barbed, and spear-shaped as other woodpeckers' tongues, which are adapted to probing in small cavities for insect food. The sapsucker's brushy tongue in perfectly suited to "lapping up" the tree sap that oozes from the numerous holes they bore into trees. The maple trees in my yard are riddled with dozens of holes, none of them more than three-eighths of an inch deep, but deep enough to have penetrated the living layer of cambium. The birds consume the nutritious cambium, as well as the sap that seeps through the holes.

As the weather begins to warm, more and more insects emerge, many of which are attracted to the dripping tree sap. This becomes the source of a good portion of the fat and protein that are also vital to the diet of the sapsuckers. Approximately 50 percent of this bird's food consists of insects; the other 50, including tree sap, comes from plants. Some people attempted to raise orphaned young sapsuckers on only diluted maple syrup, but they failed and the birds died. Upon being examined, the dead birds were found to have softened, enlarged, and poorly functioning livers resulting from a diet that was too heavy with sugar.

About 40 years ago, my dad planted two ponderosa pines in his yard. Today they have developed into beautiful trees. The one near the back of his property, next to a rock garden, has about as many sapsucker holes in it as one could possibly imagine being in one tree. It was near this tree that I trapped and banded my first yellow-bellied sapsucker. What a reception this shrill-voiced male gave me! What a tongue lashing! How I wish I had owned a tape recorder then. And his sharply curved claws were needle-pointed. But the most interesting discovery came when examining the bird's tail. Talk about a sticky, matted mess of feathers! It was obvious that the bird had been frequenting the tacky pitch dripping down the trunk of the ponderosa.

As winter ends, it gives in to some of the most beautiful and subtle animal behavior of the entire year. Try to include in your busy schedules enough time to spend a few hours each week "back in," off the beaten track, where you can sit and relax and wait for some of nature's greatest performers to tell you their story. You'll come away a better person, and you'll want to hurry back for the next performance.

Musical Larks

Shortly after the turn of this century, a group of Americans, dissatisfied with the bald eagle as our national bird, decided to do something about it. I don't know who the instigators were or what caused their plan to "fizzle," but their actions did arouse considerable sympathy from various parts of the country. Their choice to replace the bald eagle was the meadowlark.

Very likely a large number of the group's followers were from Kansas, Montana, Nebraska, North Dakota, Oregon, and Wyoming. For the western meadowlark has been chosen as the state bird by all of these states. Few other native birds are as widespread as the meadowlarks. In fact, one can expect to find them in every state except Hawaii and Alaska.

These robin-sized, stubby-tailed birds of the open fields include an eastern and a western species. Most people would have difficulty telling them apart, even using binoculars. However, once you hear their songs you will remember them for the rest of your life. The eastern meadowlark ranges from southeastern Canada to northern Mexico, west to Minnesota and Nebraska. Western meadowlarks can be found from southwestern Canada south to Mexico, east into Wisconsin and Oklahoma. Their ranges overlap only minimally, so we in eastern Wisconsin are fortunate to have both species.

Briefly, the song of the western meadowlark is a rich, mellow, descending warble that stops abruptly. The eastern meadowlark sings with a higher-pitched, smooth, piercing whistle. An experience I had a few days ago with several groups of first graders proved to me that these young children were hearing and remembering bird songs quite accurately, and that included the song of the meadowlark.

I was introducing about a dozen of our native songbirds to them using life-sized, painted plastic models of the birds. The meadowlark proved to be a favorite. After we had discussed this valuable bird and I had listened to some of the children's stories, I told them that two dif-

77

ferent kinds of meadowlarks lived in this part of the state. I said that I would whistle their songs and they were to raise their hands if they had heard one or both of them.

A small number of hands went up after hearing the eastern meadowlark's smooth easy whistle. Most of their hands shot up as I imitated the western's rich warble. The interesting thing about this episode is that the children's reactions coincided with the figures resulting from a survey of breeding birds we conduct each June in the area where quite a few of these children live.

My survey records, taken at 50 stops, each a half mile apart, over the past eight years, show the following results. Western meadowlarks heard from 1970 through 1977 were 54, 70, 50, 73, 71, 34, 45, and 43. Eastern meadowlarks heard over the same period at the same stops were 20, 28, 19, 28, 25, 14, 15 and 5. This amounts to more than twice the number of westerns as easterns in this region of northern Kewaunee and southern Door counties.

Experts tell us that the western meadowlark tends to be slightly smaller than the eastern, and to have a fuller coloration on its back. Also, the yellow on its chin extends farther up onto its cheeks. Two outstanding field marks can be seen on both: a broad V-shaped black necklace on a deep sunny lemon-yellow breast, and white outer tail feathers. Frequently one sees the meadowlark flying away. It is then that the white tail feathers are easy to spot.

A musical western meadowlark kept our Army company at Fort Sill in good humor for a couple of months one year. Each morning a highly vocal male beautifully shattered the dawn stillness as we stood at attention outside the barracks, waiting for the first sergeant to take roll call. I like to imagine it was singing. "I think I hear your company lining up." (Say the first five words slowly and the last three faster.) What a magnificent bubbling alto yodel that bird had!

Meadowlarks, with their long, strong, cone-shaped, pointed bills and flat foreheads are related to red-winged blackbirds, orioles, grackles, and starlings. One inspection of the many types of harmful insects this nervous tail-flicking bird eats would convince farmers that it is an extremely valuable friend to have around.

These birds fly low and straight with rapid wing beats—flapping, then sailing; flapping and sailing. They have a tendency to choose high perches from which to sing. Their jerky walk on relatively long legs is much like that of their relatives.

I would guess that many of you share my fondness for early summer and the thrilling sight and sound of the morning's first sun highlighting the meadowlark's breast as he faces east and serenades the meadows and the fields into awakening.

Spring Woods Percussionist

That polished master of spring woods percussion, the ruffed grouse, greets the brisk early morning scene with a muffled throbbing paradiddle. His song could very well be titled "Call of the Wild," composed expressly for drums and timpani.

Imagine the cock bird, tail fanned majestically, black feathers on the side of his throat extended into ruffs and highlighted with a brassy metallic glint by the early morning sun, strutting like a pompous little Tom turkey back and forth on an old moss-covered log. Now and then he lowers and shakes his head vigorously. Suddenly he props his tail firmly against the log and fans his wings forward with powerful bursts at a slow cadence, producing a series of dull thuds. Gradually, the thuds turn into a muffled ventriloquial roll, like gentle, far-off thunder.

Several years ago I camped at Devils Lake State Park on a weekend in mid-April, choosing a secluded campsite near the wooded base of the bluff. Just as I was getting into my sleeping bag, a group of Boy Scouts arrived from Chicago. It was already quite late so I decided to wait until morning to go over to meet them. At 5 A.M. I woke to the drumming sounds of a ruffed grouse near my tent. What a splendid concert that grandiose strutter presented!

After breakfast, I went to talk with the scouts and their leaders. One of the first things I asked them was whether any had heard the grouse earlier that morning. None of them had, but then I realized that perhaps they didn't know what the bird sounded like. Cleveland Grant, a wildlife lecturer, had once shown me how to imitate the grouse's drumming by beating on my chest with my fists.

In this way, I tried to reproduce the sound as I described the bird's performance. Finally, one of the boys' eyes lit up and he said, "Yeah, I heard that sound, but I thought it was my heart beating real loud!" Everyone laughed at his rather apt description.

Last week, when the big snowbank in our front yard finally melted, Charlotte and I discovered a dead ruffed grouse on the ground.

We suspect that it had suffered a fatal accident during the big blizzard that had occurred a month earlier. The bird's black tail band was incomplete across the two central feathers, indicating that it probably was a female. Her pectinated toes were interesting to study. Covered with fringelike scales, they serve as snowshoes during the deep snows of winter. The bottoms appeared to have efficient treads that helped her to inch her way along narrow branches of ironwood, birch, aspen, maple, willow, or cherry trees in search of buds to eat. In spring, the scales are molted.

After the female ruffed grouse has mated, she constructs a shallow nest on the ground, usually against some object, such as a log, or even a steep bank. The first grouse nest I ever saw I discovered accidentally in what I call the Christmas Fern Woods near Ellisville. It was the last week of May. I had been taking a count of Christmas ferns and was making my way up a steep slope in the hardwoods. Suddenly I stopped in my tracks and found myself staring straight at the beady black eye of a female grouse, no more than five feet in front of me, sitting on her eggs.

It was obvious that she was trusting in her marvelous camouflage to protect her. But her dark glistening eye gave her away. Admiring her great courage, I slowly took one step forward. Abruptly, and with a nerve-shattering explosion of feathered lightning, she flew from the nest, nearly knocking my hat off. I tracked her speedy exit in a long curving arc for about 80 yards as she cackled excitedly all the way. Behind her, in the nest, she left approximately a dozen creamy buff eggs.

Newborn ruffed grouse are precocial, that is, they are capable of independent activity right from birth. Indeed, they are able to scamper and find their own food as soon as they are dried off. But they are constantly and carefully watched over by the dauntless hen. Because of their many natural enemies—such as owls, hawks, snakes, cows, badgers, fox, skunks, dogs, and crows—only about 40 percent of the young survive into early September.

Research has shown that these stalwart birds consume portions of about 375 different plants—nuts, seeds, buds, blossoms, leaves, and fruits—as well as 130 small creatures and insects. The ruffed grouse in the Sanctuary especially enjoy wintergreen berries and leaves, jewelweed leaves, and the entire plants of cow wheat *(Melampyrum lineare)*.

81

The best thing we can do to ensure the survival of the ruffed grouse is to preserve a sufficient number of mixed forests laced with clearings and bordered with plenty of willows and aspens. In this way, we can also make certain that generations to come will thrill to this star performer that is native to every county in Wisconsin. Let us hope that its drum rolls will always echo through the damp air of early spring mornings, the perfect symbol of the wild outdoors.

Genius Of The Bog

By mid to late April, the American bittern—a shy, stocky wading bird of the marshes—has usually returned to Wisconsin for the nesting season. This bird has the reputation of being one of the most unusual and outlandish singers in the entire bird world. But so secretive is the American bittern that most people who hear its extraordinary song rarely see the bird who sings it.

Several years ago my dad was confined to bed while recuperating from a spinal operation. School had just ended and I was home for a visit. My students had given me a present of two fine bird-song records and I was playing them in the living room. Suddenly the bittern song began with its peculiar series of loud gutteral pumping belches. Dad recognized the sounds immediately and said that as a boy on his family's farm west of Slovan, he used to hear those strange noises coming from the pond behind the barn every spring. But since he had never seen the creature responsible for the unique sound, he presumed that it was coming from a frog of unknown species.

Dozens of phonetic renditions of the bittern's song have been committed to paper. Invariably the first syllable is indicated as being drawn out. The middle sound is short and quite sharp. And the last part of the song is somewhat lower than the first and not quite as long. Use your imagination and attempt to hear the song in your mind: "Ung-ka-gunk, oonck-a-tsoonk, oong-ka-choonk, pump-er-lunk, dunk-a-doo, chunk-a-lunk, umph-ta-googh, pung-ka-chuck, kung-ka-unk."

My first experience with the American bittern occurred while a friend and I, using an old dilapidated third-hand canoe, explored the marshy sloughs that border the Kewaunee River. As we rounded a mirror-calm bend in the river, we surprised a bittern wading along the shore in search of food. Startled, it gave out a loud croaking "squawk" and, with faster than normal wing beats, flew off in a huff, legs and feet dangling, defecating a stream of chalky white excrement as it departed. As straitlaced and serious as this old "poker face" bird appears to be, I can imagine him laughing with glee after scaring us out of our wits.

Upon telling our story at the sporting goods store, some of the old hunting cronies informed us that we had seen a ''shitepoke.'' During the ensuing years I learned that a shitepoke is one of various herons and bitterns who habitually defecate when they are flushed from cover.

The bittern makes its home in reedy marshes, where bulrushes, cattails, sedges, and tall grasses grow. For that reason, this inconspicuous loner is seen mostly by people who spend a lot of time in the field and are not afraid to get their feet wet.

Alexander ''Sandy'' Sprunt, an instructor at the Wisconsin Audubon Camp near Sarona, taught me a valuable lesson that has helped me learn more about nature. One day he took our class to a secluded little hillside that bordered a tiny marsh located within a block or two of a shallow lake. There we were instructed to sit quietly, wait, and watch carefully. Finally, he looked at his watch and said, ''Within the next two or three minutes you are going to see an American bittern fly to the corner of the marsh directly to our left front.'' His prediction was accurate. For through patient and daily observation, he had learned the habits of that bittern and, just as though he had ''staged'' it, the bird appeared. Sandy had just let nature come to him.

The plumage of this wading bird is said to be cryptic. For with brown streaks on a whitish breast and a spearlike beak that thrusts skyward, it blends easily with its reedy environment. One can imagine this creature, confident in its camouflage, allowing an observer to approach quite closely. Then, with his usual bad manners, the audacious bittern gives his ''shitepoke'' reception and bids a speedy farewell!

When airborne, the bittern holds its neck in the typical heron S-shape, but has quicker wing beats and a smoother flight than the larger herons. Its serious-appearing, ''no nonsense'' eyes are angled considerably downward on the sides of its head. Thus, when the bird strikes its ''alert'' pose, bill pointed straight upward, both eyes can focus upon any intruders.

I had a memorable experience with a bittern during a Thanksgiving vacation while I was a college student. The river had frozen early that year enabling me to take a shortcut to my favorite woods north of Kewaunee, where a tiny creek bordered with rushes emptied. I was just about to jump over the creek when a large bird, practically beneath my feet, lunged at me, puffed up its feathers, and gave me a scare to remember. It turned out to be an injured bittern, unable to fly and

Charlotte Lukes

American Bittern

searching for food in the trickle of water.

Several years later I experienced a more pleasant surprise when I accidentally stumbled onto a nest of half-grown bitterns. They ran and hid with ease, but after some searching, I succeeded in locating one of them. What a sight it was: ungainly, and messy-looking, a baby that only a mother bittern could love. And when I picked him up, the young heron proved to be quite unfriendly. First, it defecated; then it regurgitated; and finally, in despair, it lunged at me repeatedly with its beak, all in an attempt to make me release it. It was difficult to believe that this desperate bundle of feathers would someday develop an art of hiding that would foil the experts and an exotic song that would please the ear. But given a little time, this young bittern, like many before him, was sure to grow into what Thoreau described as the "genius of the bog."

Spring Bird Wishing

A dreadfully wintry May 6 wind swept in from the northeast last night and surprised us with a trace of snow. The birds in the yard are on edge, partly as a result of the high winds and partly because of my simple old-fashioned drop trap, set and triggered primarily for a banded red-winged blackbird I want so much to catch. As I write this, I have one eye on the trap (triggered by a fish line leading from the window) and the other eye on my paper.

Good luck! In practically no time, I have a blue jay in the trap. A few seconds more, using an old homemade butterfly net, and I have the jay safely in hand. The band, numbered 763-01525, will accompany her for the rest of her days. Depending upon the direction of her migratory flights, and many other factors, she may help us to learn more about her species.

Usually, it is next to impossible to determine the sex of a blue jay from its outward appearance. But this one sported a large-sized incubation patch on her underside. Although the patch is covered by feathers, I merely blew firmly on her belly and revealed it. I know one thing for sure. From now on, she will keep a safe distance from the cracked corn and sunflower seeds, the bait, lying beneath the raised trap.

Just minutes ago, a brown thrasher inched under the trap for some corn. I pulled the string, but ''Brownie'' was quite alert and left me with empty hands. To my surprise the thrasher is now up on the beef suet feeder pulling bits and pieces away and eating them. Unlike the woodpecker—which has a third brace, its tail, to help hold firmly onto the feeder—the thrasher appears awkward as it balances on the narrow shelf.

Several days ago, while discussing bird stories (and proper people behavior) at school, one of my students came out with the usual: ''And my mommy said that you should never touch the bird's eggs or babies or else the mother bird will never return to take care of them.'' Although I always agree, that it *is* a good idea to stay well away from nests for fear of leading predators to them, the story that I told in response to these young students contradicted the popular belief.

The parent bird, frequently the female, has a brood patch of bare inflamed skin on her belly that is very warm to the touch. Blood vessels close to the surface of this brood patch cause her to be uncomfortable when away from her eggs. The longer she is away, the more eager she is to return, quite likely in order to lower herself onto the smooth cool eggs. In fact, I suspect that the reason some birds regularly turn their eggs is to expose the cool sides to the top, hence bringing soothing comfort to their hot, irritating brood patch.

What a phenomenon of precision and beauty, that nature should provide birds with a built-in regulator forcing the mother bird to sit on the eggs so her body heat will cause them to hatch. I often wonder if the female bird laying eggs for the first time has any awareness that baby birds will hatch from them!

*   *   *

We are worried about the rose-breasted grosbeaks. In 1973, the first ones arrived on April 22. Therefore, they are already two weeks late, according to that date. I hate to think that they might have been caught by some of the destructive tornadoes that tore through mid-America a few weeks ago. Time will tell.

Most of the other bird arrivals are pretty much on time when compared with other years. The first whippoorwill sang out in the tag alders, along with the spring peepers, last Friday, May 3. Our first (and always the earliest) nesting warbler, the northern waterthrush, carolled lustily in the backyard Sunday.

Dozens of purple finches come to our feeders daily, adding their melodius warbling to the music of the great outdoors. We patiently wait for the catbird, wood thrush, ruby-throated hummingbird, Baltimore oriole, and, above all, the rose-breasted grosbeaks. Their color; their smooth, easy, rich songs; and their trust that allows me to approach them so closely make them pretty much our summer favorites.

*   *   *

But I'm daydreaming. I'd better concentrate on catching that banded red-winged blackbird. You know the old saying: ''A bird in the hand is worth two in the bush!''

87

Spirit Lifter

In spite of sunny skies, a gusty northeaster was playing tricks on a large number of rose-breasted grosbeaks—at least 16—feeding in our backyard. With some regularity, the wind blew the sunflower seeds off the platform feeders and onto the ground. And occasionally it got so strong that it blasted the birds themselves off their feeding perches. The grosbeaks soon realized that the best feeding was to be had on the ground.

As I watched those dignified birds today, I remembered the first rose-breasted grosbeaks I ever saw. I was with about 230 explorer scouts and several of their dads on a weekend campout, west of Madison, in early May of 1956. Our destination was a scenic, wooded valley in Wyoming Township, Iowa County, about 10 miles beyond Arena.

The dads and I laid out our sleeping bags on the floor of an old abandoned farmhouse. The boys, all seventh and eighth graders, wanted to be by themselves. I recall those youngsters and realize how competent and trustworthy they were, thoroughly enjoying the various responsibilities of setting up their camp, and succeeding in making it well-arranged, neat and orderly.

We were far enough away from the narrow gravel road so that we were not disturbed by the noise of passing cars. This was the valley of the whippoorwills, and in the stillness of that first night the birds sounded as though they were directly overhead.

The next morning, a bird song that was new to most of us flooded the valley. I was able to identify it as the song of the rose-breasted grosbeak. And so alluring was the continuous concert that we decided to see if we could locate the singer. We found it difficult to believe that so much beauty could come from the throat of one bird. Its flowing phrases and slurs, its variety of notes, and its rolling warbles completely captivated us. Since then, I have had many experiences with the rose-breasted grosbeaks, but I will never forget the thrill of that first encounter.

Later on that morning one of our "snake experts" located a large hognosed snake under the bridge that spanned a tiny creek near our camp. How vicious it acted one minute, and how tormented and suffering the next. First it coiled and hissed, then it turned over on its back and played dead.

A typical campfire ended our day, and we "old codgers" headed for the farmhouse, which was about 300 yards away, while the scouts "sacked out" in their tents. It had been a perfect day, ushered in by rose-breasted grosbeaks and serenaded to an end by whippoorwills.

At about midnight, however, we were abruptly jolted out of our sleeping bags by a genuine, old-fashioned "gully-washer" of a storm accompanied by lightning and booming thunder. Our first thought was to put on our rain gear, take our lanterns, and get out to see how the boys and their tents were withstanding the storm. They weren't. They hadn't trenched their tents, which were leaking badly, and all were trying to get to the farmhouse with their soggy sleeping bags as quickly as they could.

I don't know why we didn't do a head count at the boys' camp, but when we got back to the farmhouse we discovered that one boy was missing. We hadn't realized how well Bruce had concealed his tent. So, back again out into the storm we went. When we finally found him we nearly went into hysterics of laughter, with the ridiculous appearance of his tiny pup tent sagging so low in the pelting rain that it was touching the boy, who was snoring contentedly, totally unaware of the storm!

The grosbeaks awakened us to a sunny morning and their songs soon warmed our dampened spirits. I wondered where those high-class birds had wintered. Later I learned that many of them do so in the forested hills of Guatemala and Panama, spending about five months down south, five up here, and the remainder enroute. People in Central America commonly trap rose-breasted grosbeaks and cage them for their beauty and song. Fortunately, laws prohibit that practice in this country.

A few of the grosbeaks at our feeders yesterday carried bands on their right legs. Most likely they are the numbered government bands I placed there last year or before. Once again I will attempt to trap as many as I can for study purposes. Perhaps the eventual result of all of the various banding efforts that are made along its range will be to unlock at least some of the secrets of this colorful bird's migratory patterns. It would be both interesting and instructive to know the exact route it follows.

The word "grosbeak" can be traced to the French *gros bec*, meaning fat bill. In all likelihood one or more of the group that I will be studying will clamp its fantastically strong beak onto one of my fingers and practically bring me to me knees in painful payment for having disturbed it. However, in no way will this lessen my extreme fondness for these summer favorites.

Nesting grosbeaks are devoted parents. Both male and female participate in the construction of the nest, the incubation of the eggs, and the feeding of the young, who consume many harmful insects, such as cutworms, tent caterpillars, and potato bugs. Perhaps the excellence of the grosbeak parenting is the reason why the cowbird frequently chooses it to rear its young.

Beauty of plumage, richness of song, devotion to their young, destroyer of injurious insect pests—the rose-breasted grosbeak has it all! What more could we possibly expect from a bird?

Owl Talk

On a recent spring day, I worked with a group of primary school children examining life-sized plastic bird models and listening to recorded bird songs. As in all other similar classes, none of the birds received more instant recognition nor created more excitement than the screech owl. Later that day George Pederson, a science teacher at the junior high school, asked me if I had seen the owl pellets on the ground beneath the huge hemlock tree in the school forest. Fortunately there hadn't been any recent hard rains and several pellets were still intact, brimming with tiny bones.

Naturally I had owls on my mind as my wife, our friends Jim and Libby Zimmerman, and I went outdoors that evening to enjoy the woodcock's concert in the back meadow. We had no sooner positioned ourselves in the area to the south of the grove of aspen trees than the clamorous "hoot owl's" calls split the night air in the swale to our backs: "Who cooks for YOU? Who cooks for YOU alll?" After a bit of this, we realized that, somewhere out there in the dark, a spooky conversation was going on between two, and possibly three, owls. Suddenly we heard a single, loud, "WHOOOK," and Charlotte leaned over and whispered, "Do you suppose that owl was goosed?"

I spent the next morning carefully dissecting the owl pellets on my basement workbench. It is amazing what one can learn from such an exercise. I strongly suspect the two-inch-long, elliptical, matted balls of undigestible fur, feathers (very few), and bones that George had showed me had been coughed up by one or more great horned owls. A few of the hollow, round bones were nearly a quarter-inch wide. The majority were very small, however, and included the jawbones of more than a half dozen field mice. One jawbone resembled that of a chipmunk. Actually, the great horned owl has quite a diversified diet that might include the following: chipmunk, flying squirrel, cottontail, meadow mouse, shrew, skunk, blue jay, flicker, screech owl, domestic chicken, pigeon, snake, ruffed grouse, porcupine, dog, and cat.

I marveled at how ivory-clean the bones in the pellets were. Strong digestive juices of that "flying tiger" had dissolved every trace of meat.

Even though few people ever see a live horned owl, Fran Hamerstrom, an expert on predatory birds, believes that this species breeds in more North American counties than any other bird.

Several years ago, two dead owls were brought to me: one was a 16-inch barred owl, found by my neighbor in back of his garage; the other was a 7-inch saw-whet owl, discovered dead against a chicken-wire fence by a former student. Comparative examination of the owls proved to be interesting. The size of their ears was downright startling. Concealed beneath the feathers on the sides of their heads were their "ear horns." These projected outward from *the front* of surprisingly wide auditory canals—not from *the back*, as on humans.

The facial discs that surrounded their eyes, like miniature parabolic reflectors, were things of beauty. These reflectors help to concentrate sounds, thereby enabling the owls, even in total darkness, to strike with nearly unerring accuracy.

The barred owl's eyes are equally amazing. Their size, in proportion to the animal's total body weight, puts them near the head of the list of large-eyed creatures. The increased eye dimensions produce a large, razor-sharp image on the retinas, a vital factor in the success of these nocturnal hunters. Surprisingly these color-blind birds have "eye-shine," as do many other animals, so that in the beam of a flashlight their black, somber eyes appear red.

Most people do not realize that some owls, such as the tiny saw-whets, occasionally are migratory. Friends of mine—Bernard Brouchoud, of Manitowoc, and Tom Erdman, of Green Bay—have trapped and banded a considerable number in cooperation with the U.S. Fish and Wildlife Service. In fact, Bernie captured 133 in one season. I was quite surprised the first time I observed Bernie release a saw-whet. After receiving its band, the bird fluttered up to a tall maple tree like a woodcock or giant-sized bumblebee. There it sat and stared at us for a long time.

Tom Erdman caught a saw-whet in one of his mist nets one day when my wife and I were observing his banding operations. After he had banded and studied the bird, he asked if I would like to photograph it. Naturally I agreed, and got ready for the quick picture I would snap the split second he set the bird free. "Take your time," Tom said,

"I'll just set him on this branch and you can take all the pictures you want. He'll sit there watching you."

Tom was right. Finally I moved to within about 20 inches of the patient little bird. To this day, I still wonder who was more interested in whom! And I was reminded of that grand old proverb, "A wise old owl sat in an oak, the more he saw the less he spoke, the less he spoke the more he heard, why can't we all be like that wise old bird?"

Butterfly Birds

Last Saturday, while my wife and I worked in the garden, we were treated to an unforgettable bird experience. Our pleasure was probably heightened all the more becuase we were busily involved in the unenjoyable task of digging out last fall's neglected weeds.

We had commented several times during the previous week about the late arrival of the rose-breasted grosbeaks. So far only one male and one female had appeared at the feeders and it was already May 10. But then on Saturday, suddenly, and with an excited flurry of song, they were there. Seemingly coming out of nowhere, a flock of grosbeaks alighted high in the maples singing lustily. Their rollicking happy music flowed through the yard as though they were saying: "The troops have arrived. Get out the sunflower seeds!"

Later that day, as Charlotte was preparing supper, she received yet another surprise. "New bird at the feeders," she shouted. "Red-bellied woodpecker!" We watched the new bird, a beautiful male, as he sat on the east platform feeder, feasting on sunflower seeds. When a careless jay got one inch too close, the "redbelly" made a lunging jab at him, reminding the jay that he was not a bird to be toyed with. We hoped he would decide to return often.

Francis Lee Jaques, a famous bird artist, once remarked, "The difference between warblers and no warblers is very slight." Larger, slower moving birds, such as ducks and herons, were his favorite subjects. But many birders, on the other hand, wait with great anticipation for the spring arrival of these "butterflies of the bird world."

Fifty-four species of these small, flighty, difficult-to-identify birds nest north of the Mexican border. In fact warblers comprise about one-half of the bird population of Canada's vast evergreen forest. Perhaps the reason that most people take little interest in these elusive creatures is that they are generally inconspicuous and downright difficult to study even when you do get a good look at them.

Mother's Day of 1961, May 13, is recorded in my field notes as a superb day for warblers. As bird students would say, the warbler wave was on. Tiny tree leaves were just unfolding, the air was warm, and tens of thousands of gnats were hatching, providing an abundance of food for the hungry birds.

I remember the day as vividly as though it were yesterday, for it was then that I saw my first male black-throated blue warbler—as well as my second, my third, and my fourth. They fed low in the big Norway spruce tree in my folks' backyard, and they allowed me to get within 8 or 10 feet of them. By the end of that remarkable backyard birding day, I had seen 19 species of warblers in addition to about 40 other species.

During the first part of May, one of the Midwest's most fantastic spots for sighting warblers is Wyalusing State Park, located near Prairie du Chien, at the confluence of the Wisconsin and Mississippi Rivers. Two friends and I camped there on the weekend of May 10-11, 1958, in quest of warblers. Our camp happened to be near that of a group of Beloit college students and their biology professor, and on Friday night, while sitting around the campfire, we mentioned to the professor the purpose of our being in the park.

"How would you like to see a prothonotary warbler tomorrow morning?" he asked. Surely he knew what we'd say. In fact it would be a first sighting for two of us. He gave us letter-perfect directions for locating a specific tree at the edge of one of the bayous. And he was so positive the bird would be there, he was willing to bet us a twenty dollar bill we'd see it. To this day, I marvel at his directions and the thrill we experienced the following morning when, indeed, we did see the flashy prothonotary.

Undoubtedly, spring is the best time to study and, especially, to begin mastering warbler identification. Warblers in fall plumage are even more difficult to identify. Don't overlook their songs as valuable aids in identification. The Ontario Federation of Naturalists produces a phonograph record containing excellent warbler songs.

Much to our pleasure, the annual convention of the National Audubon Society was held in Milwaukee several years ago. Prior to the convention, Murl Deusing and Joe Schneider organized a tour into Door County to do some birding. I don't know if these people cast some sort of spell over our area or whether they merely were good positive thinkers, but so help me, while they were here there were warblers in practically every tree and bush in the county! Talk about a bunch of happy birders.

One can expect to find the following warblers, each in its own environmental niche, nesting in our region: black and white, golden-winged, blue-winged, Nashville, parula, yellow, Myrtle, blackburnian, chestnut-sided, pine, oven-bird, northern waterthrush, yellow-throat, and American redstart. This list is not meant to be complete. Once you match these warbler names with their pictures and their habitats there is no way you can resist being lured into the actual search for these captivating ''butterflies of the bird world.''

Mimics

The handsome, skittish brown thrasher in our backyard prompted me to have the kindergarten children with whom I am working make up their own names for a few of the bird models we've been discussing. One of my favorite names came from a little girl who called a goldfinch a "sunbird."

Our thrasher has been living up to its name quite well, sweeping its head from side to side in search of food and scattering debris on the ground as it does so. And when it does locate something edible, living or otherwise, it attacks it vigorously.

The head and back of the thrasher are a dazzling light cinnamon color and its whitish underparts are streaked with dark brown. What captivates us most, in addition to its song, is the fierce determined look in its flashy yellow eyes. It always looks as though it means business.

The few times we've heard this hearty vocalist singing back in the tag alders it sounded as though it was just getting warmed up for the real songs to follow, frequently repeating its phrases twice with clarity and power.

Unlike its somewhat more trusting mimic relatives, the catbird and the mockingbird, the thrasher appears to be very shy and vanishes at the slightest noise or disturbance. But if you should happen to approach its nest too closely, it becomes angry and fearless.

Thirty-one species of mockingbirds, catbirds, and thrashers live in the Americas, most of them in Mexico. Of these, the mockingbird—that champion mimic—is claimed as the "number-one" bird by five states.

What a thrill I had when I saw my first mockingbird. It was late in the spring of 1954, at about 6:00 in the evening, and I was on my way to one of the small civilian-run laundries at Fort Sill, Oklahoma. I was walking, as usual, taking a shortcut through an undeveloped section of the camp. The skeleton remains of many large, old, wooden tent frames were clustered in the middle of a field. As I was crossing the field with a bag of dirty laundry over my back, I suddenly and literally was stopped in my tracks by a fantastic outpouring of bird music.

It didn't take long to locate the ambitious singer. Entranced by the unexpected concert, I tossed my laundry bag to the ground, sat up against one of the old tent frames, and the two of us—the mockingbird and I—shared the whisper-quiet evening, with him doing all the "talking" and me the listening.

The mimic that we most enjoyed at home from the time I was a boy, was the sleek, gray, friendly catbird. My dad, who frequently rose early on summer mornings to work in the garden, claimed that the catbird appeared to enjoy human company and would often come close to him in search of breakfast.

Catbirds lack the loud clarity of the mockingbird and brown thrasher but are, nevertheless, interesting singers. They don't mimic or repeat their phrases, but their mewing catcalls are unmistakable. And the catbird, like the other true mimics, is aggressive and inquisitive. For the sake of experiment, I once challenged a catbird by vigorously kissing the back of my hand to make a threatening, squeaking, teasing call. The catbird, instead of fleeing at the sound, boldly approached to within several feet of me. Should a similar scolding distress call be given by a "real" bird, the catbird would be one of the first to arrive, perhaps to help in driving some intruder out of its territory.

The more I study and observe the mimics, the more I admire them. Aristocrats of song, backyard nightingales, and fearless individualists, they are also willing to help a neighbor, easy-to-get-along-with, and scrupulously clean "housekeepers." We humans would do well, indeed, to mimic the mimics.

Rewards Of Birding

Up in one of the maple trees outside my window a yellow-shafted flicker is making a racket. It is a male and he's perched on top of the thick stub of a large branch that broke off the tree several years ago. The branch just happens to contain a perfect nesting cavity for a flicker. And, my guess is that that's what this bird has in mind.

*   *   *

Anyone who has ever had flickers nesting in his yard has probably had to put up with their unpredictable and often unwelcome antics. I can remember times during my childhood when flickers would attack the metal vent pipe on top of our roof. The attack generally took place at about five in the morning. Whatever possesses flickers to do this kind of thing, I don't know. It might be some form of territorial behavior; or perhaps they are releasing their frustrations by banging away at whatever hard metal object they can get at.

*   *   *

This spring I watched the American goldfinches go through their prenuptial molt. Nearly all of the males are now in their brilliant yellow and black plumage. But they were quite forlorn looking while they were molting! It was especially interesting to observe the varying rates at which the changes took place in this flock of 30 or 40 birds. Some had just begun to show a little yellow when others had nearly completed their change.

*   *   *

The spring's first rufous-sided towhee, a flashy male, presented himself this morning as I ate breakfast. Whenever I see this bird, I always think: Here is a real "thoroughbred." What class! Every move it makes displays its best features. Its tail is especially expressive as the towhee goes about its business of scratching among the leaves and grass for food. And its ''drink-your-tea-ee-ee-ee'' song is one of the most interesting of all bird songs.

A blue jay stands this minute, its back toward me, several feet away on one of the narrow perches of the Koenig feeder. It uses its tail for balance as it grasps a sunflower seed between its feet and hammers away with its bill, trying to get at the meat of the seed. Should he ever

*   *   *

miss the seeds, I wonder if he might not end up with a bruised toe. For this bird is no weakling, as you will readily observe if you ever hold one in your hands. Now he senses my presence, hurriedly gulps down three or four seeds, and flies over to the little spruce next to the garage where he continues his breakfast undisturbed.

The day I learned the blue jay's ''pump handle'' call was a day I shall never forget. I was rooming with a family on the west side of Madison. A tiny elderly lady who lived across the narrow street from us got up bright and early every morning to draw a pail of water from her outdoor well. The well had an old-fashioned pump and, like many old pumps, it had a delightful bit of rusty music to accompany its action. Morning after morning I could hear her at the pump. One day, as I was enjoying the early morning sun, elbows propped upon the window sill, the pump suddenly began to sing by itself—and the handle wasn't moving. Ghosts!! Was I dreaming? Right about then the ventriloquist moved and revealed himself. It wasn't the pump at all. It was an ordinary old blue jay. For weeks I had been giving the little old lady credit for the beautiful morning music. But I was wrong. Naturally this song has come to be one of my favorites.

Champion Plover

Our friend Tom pulled into the driveway just before supper last night, banged on the back door, and hollered: "There are 30 whimbrels feeding on the mud flats at the head of the bay. Do you want to see them?"

Oh how I groaned to myself. I had been swinging a spiking hammer and post maul all day and had just settled down into a tub of hot water to soothe my aching muscles. I called to Charlotte and said that she should take a camera and a long lens and go with Tom.

They returned about 45 minutes later bursting with excitement. The birds had cooperated and allowed them to get some good pictures. These transient shorebirds are rarely seen in Wisconsin, so the sighting was a real stroke of good fortune. Then, as an added bonus, Charlotte and Tom accidentally flushed a killdeer off its nest and were able to pinpoint its location.

We returned to the shore of the bay today and, as we had expected, found that the whimbrels had left. But as long as we had come this far, we decided to have a look at the killdeer nest before heading back home. Noisy red-winged blackbirds and grackles worked the shores of the creek nearby in search of food. They appeared to be quite unconcerned about our presence as we slowly and cautiously passed them on our way to the nesting site.

Charlotte described objects to look for: a small shrub and, to its left, a leaning light-gray stick. Her directions were perfect. There the nervous killdeer sat as both of us, using binoculars, studied its reaction to our approach. By the time we had come to within 35 yards of this robin-sized plover, it was up and running, sounding its excited rattling alarm call.

Suddenly the long-legged killdeer spread its wings, fanned out its cinnamon-colored tail, flopped onto its side and became the most tortured, injured, forlorn creature one could possibly imagine. The bird's "condition" worsened as we walked directly toward the nest. Now we purposely changed our direction and walked somewhat away from the nest and toward the fluttering adult. But the bird was on its feet and well in less than a second, leading us on a merry chase away from its precious eggs.

The more our pace quickened, the faster the killdeer ran. In fact, its movements were so gyroscopically smooth that it looked as though it was moving on wheels rather than on legs. Finally, after at least three minutes of this wild killdeer chase, a second killdeer appeared, obviously the first bird's mate. The second bird now took up the broken wing act while the first snuggled down onto the ground, perhaps trying to get us to believe that it was sitting on its nest and that's where we should come to look for its eggs if that was what we were after.

Undoubtedly, more Americans are familiar with the killdeer than any other shorebird. Both its easily recognized "kill-DEE, kill-DEE" call and the two bold black stripes on its white breast are good field marks. In flight, this popular creature reveals a long tail, buffy cinnamon top, and slender pointed wings. A scope or binoculars are needed to see its handsome red eye rings.

A killdeer usually lays four eggs in its nest which, in all likelihood, will be little more than a slight depression in the ground. The nests we've inspected recently had tiny bits of dried grass stems for linings. The rather pointed eggs are a dull olive color liberally marked with dark brownish-black blotches. The adults take turns incubating the eggs.

The incubation period for the eggs is about 25 days, approximately twice that of robins. Even though the two birds are about the same size, the eggs of the robin are considerably smaller. The robin's young, when hatched, must be fed for a few weeks before they can leave the nest. They are said to be altricial; that is, they are hatched in a very immature condition and must be taken care of for some time. Killdeer young can run and follow their parents within minutes after hatching. Like chickens and ducks, they are precocial.

Killdeers rank high among birds that are beneficial to man, for harmful insects, such as beetles, grasshoppers, ants, and flies, make up much of their diet.

The earliest bird experience that I can remember occurred when I was just a boy; it involved a killdeer. Because one of these classy, banded plovers had nested between two rows of peas in our garden, I had many opportunities to observe it. I was thoroughly impressed by the bird's repertoire of piercing calls, exciting injury-feigning acts, its boldly marked plumage, and its effortless skimming flight. Since then, killdeers have ranked high on my list of favorite birds. And indeed, no other shorebird can ever come close to claiming its title of America's number one plover.

Sky Patrol

Which bird flies more than a thousand miles northward each spring, trusting that there will be an abundance of insects, as well as bird houses constructed by people, to ensure its survival? Entire cities honor and even advertise this graceful flier. I call it America's premier streamlined aerial socializer, the purple martin.

This bird has been attracted to sites of human habitation since the time before Columbus arrived in 1492. Accounts tell of American Indians attracting purple martins with hollowed-out bottle gourds. And one after another example has proven that martins and people—each through their own efforts—benefit each other. In fact, if an equal amount of effort and research were applied to attracting other species of insect-eating birds, millions of tons of pesticides might be eliminated annually from the environment.

These colonial nesters are the largest of the American swallows. Adult males in the spring of their third year are a dark, glossy purplish-blue. Their wings and tail are a dull black. Males beginning their second year still retain their lighter breast feathers and frequently are confused with the female martins—but not, I must add, by the female of the species.

The martins' bills, which are slightly hooked at the top, are short, broad, and triangular. Martins have an unusually wide gape which provides them with great insect-catching ability while on the wing. Watching them awkwardly maneuver on the ground, one becomes aware of their short, weak legs and feet. The martin house at my parents' home in Kewaunee is situated in the garden. As a boy, I frequently watched the martins waddle on the ground in search of nesting material or insects, especially during periods of extremely cold weather when the insects were also grounded.

Banding studies have proven that martins will quite commonly return to the same house in successive years. In fact, their homing ability is truly remarkable. One of these skillful fliers was removed from its nest box in northern Michigan, taken by automobile at night 234 miles south, and released into a completely overcast sky. The next morning, 8 hours and 35 minutes later, the bird was back in its nest box.

Some people claim that purple martins have no definite, well-structured song. In fact, a few "cranks" are so crotchety, they actually claim to despise the constant gurgling of these tireless creatures. But I call their song the sweetest music imaginable. Give me a lively colony of chattering martins any day over a highway of belching, backfiring, smelly cars and trucks.

These friendly, peaceful birds have gentle ways and are usually tolerant of people. As a result, they qualify as champions of the birdhouses. Years ago, before America was settled, the purple martins nested in hollow trees, old woodpecker holes, or even cavities in cliffs. But during the last 300 years or more, Americans have gradually perfected martin houses, realizing what valuable creatures these birds are. Indeed, more than one farmer has learned that martins chase crows and hawks from their barnyard.

A number of cities in the United States have encouraged people to construct and maintain nest boxes for purple martins. One community noted for this action is Griggsville, Illinois. The Griggsville Wild Bird Society has even gained worldwide fame. Other cities where purple martins have helped considerably to replace chemical pesticides are Fort Smith, Arkansas, Bass Lake, Indiana, Lenox, South Dakota, and Cape May, New Jersey.

As for the story that one purple martin can eat 2,000 mosquitoes in one day—I accept that with a grain of salt. Martins do consume unbelievable quantities of insect pests. On the other hand I contend that the martins may actually have little if any effect on mosquitoes in certain areas, or may even contribute to their increase. I have watched many purple martins "hawking" on the wing over the swales in the sanctuary. Their main food at times, as far as I could observe, is dragonflies. It is quite a sight to see the martins repeatedly return to several large apartment-type nest boxes along the shore with their beaks crammed full of dragonflies. And since mosquitoes are one of the main foods of dragonflies, it follows that the fewer dragonflies there are, the more mosquitoes there will be. However, this fact does not diminish my admiration and respect for these fine birds.

I tend to believe that white nest boxes are most beneficial to martins because the compartments remain cooler on hot days. And research indicates that shiny metal interiors tend to discourage starlings from using the boxes. One of our friends who had great success with his colonies of martins claimed that several ''tricks of the trade'' helped to attract dozens of them back to his houses each year. His nest boxes were always taken down and thoroughly cleaned at the end of the season, then ''sweetened'' with a few drops of oil of anise. And the houses were not erected until just prior to the arrival of the first martin scouts.

Factors that may be detrimental to the success of martins include harsh weather, drought, excessive rains and fewer insects, extreme heat resulting in dehydration of eggs or young in the nest, and persistent competitive starlings and house sparrows. If you want to help the purple martins, use your ingenuity, read books on attracting birds, and request information from special interest groups such as the Griggsville Wild Bird Society. Your efforts will be rewarded by those masters of flight, nature's best controllers of insects and gentle friends of man, the peaceful, precious purple martins.

The Orange Lover

Recently, two birds have been competing with the robins in our backyard for the "early bird" title. One is a crested flycatcher and the other, a Baltimore oriole. The flycatcher sings a monotonous, lazy, slurred "wheep" song over and over that reminds me of a sleep-robbing experience I once endured for about six weeks at Fort Sill, Oklahoma.

I had been assigned a bed on the second floor of our barracks, next to the corner windows. I considered myself fortunate because there I would enjoy more cooling breezes than the others in the barracks. But the assignment backfired. For every morning, at about 3:30 A.M., a bird perched right outside my window in one of the Chinese elms and let loose with a loud, raucous up-the-scale song that was usually ended by me stumbling downstairs in the dark, picking up a handful of gravel and flinging it up into the tree to silence the alarm clock. Sometimes it worked; most often it did not.

The other purely musical early riser in the yard here in Wisconsin is the Baltimore oriole. One can hardly get angry being awakened by this charmer, for his is a golden-throated introduction to the morning.

Orioles appear to be up in numbers this year. This could result from several factors: a better food supply last summer, more favorable weather conditions that resulted in a lower nesting mortality rate, less hazardous migratory flight conditions, and improved winter food finding. And it's possible that there is another factor that might be affecting their numbers in our area. It is known that orioles prefer to nest in live American elm trees. Perhaps the great decrease of elms to the south of us is causing more orioles to search elsewhere for suitable nesting sites.

When it comes to brilliantly colored plumage, the male Baltimore oriole is second to none. Once the male gets to be three or four years old, his orange feathers practically glow. Little wonder this bird has become such a popular and beloved bird wherever it nests.

107

Few other birds can match the female oriole in nest making. Her skillful weaving produces such well-built nests that it is not uncommon for one of them to survive three or four years of winds and storms.

The warp of the woven masterpiece usually begins with strings suspended on a drooping branch. Once the framework is completed, the female oriole begins to weave into it hundreds of long fibrous strands of plant material or anything she can find resembling plant fibers, such as yarn or string. Nearly every nest I have ever seen has been gray in color. One exception was discovered next to a horse farm where black-tailed quarter horses were being raised. This particular nest was made entirely from the long black tail hairs of the quarter horses and was an object of Black Beauty!

Generally the nests are entered from the top. However, I have seen several nests with what appeared to be an additional side entrance. It occurred to me that, with the nests as deep as they are, this side entrance might really be a peephole—a window for the adult to look through while incubating the eggs.

It seems appropriate that the orange-colored orioles would be attracted to orange food. And, indeed, they relish oranges cut in half and punched over a nail or a hook. My folks soon learned that the birds could just as readily be attracted to little cups of syrup, too. A small platform feeder with a bright orange roof, stocked with an old muffin tin containing dark syrup, attracts orioles to their yard all summer long.

What an honor Lord Baltimore received when one of our most brilliant and artistic songbirds, singer deluxe, was named after him. And so, too, do we deem it an honor to number ourselves among the fortunate people who have orioles brightening their summer yards and their lives.

Raspberry Bird

For the past several days, purple finches have been abundant at my feeders. Or should I say raspberry finches? Purple, I think, is not an appropriate name for them. Every time I see the male of this species I am reminded of ripe raspberries.

Some years ago my mother, grandmother, and I were sitting under the shade of some apple trees in our backyard, right next to the birdbath. Suddenly, with a splash, a brilliant little bird landed smack in the middle of the water. It was my grandmother who laughingly wondered aloud if that little sparrow had fallen into some raspberry juice.

Do not be too quick, as I was, to identify all of the heavily streaked brown-and-tan finches as females. As a matter of fact, banding has proven that males in their first summer of adult plumage—or, in other words, during their second year—are identical to females. The brown-and-tan finches you might see at your feeders could be either females of any age or second-year males.

I recall how sore my fingers were after banding about 180 of these birds in one day. These little rascals have quite a bite! But perhaps you and I would do the same if we were in their feathers. Their strong, heavy beaks also make them adept at cracking open sunflower seeds. My friends the Koenigs, of Sauk City, Wisconsin, in one winter's time, fed these birds 3,000 pounds of sunflower seeds. When they talk about it they always say a ton and a half—sounds like more!

The purple finch nests in our area. Its sweet, rather garbled song is quite unmistakable—different from any other bird song except, perhaps, that of the warbling vireo.

Several years ago I had the good fortune of banding almost 600 purple finches in the early spring. They had been coming to the feeders of some friends of mine north of Green Bay. One male banded on March 23 was recaptured 61 days later in Prince George, British Columbia! Check your atlas. That's quite a flight, considering the terrain the tiny creature had to fly over. To this day, it stands as my most exciting return in banding.

The evening grosbeaks are still coming to our feeders, too. I am wishfully hoping that some will remain to nest here this year. It would be a first as far as I know. The Baileys Harbor area is just right for this bird of the boreal forest, even though it is a couple hundred miles south of its usual range.

Another boreal forest nester we have in the Ridges area is the parula warbler. This bird prefers to nest in the hanging bunches of Usnea lichen (Old Man's Beard). Its song is buzzy and very high— much like an insect's call. Sizable flocks of these unusually tame birds have been seen on peoples' lawns during the past week. Stormy weather, such as we've been having lately, will cause birds to bunch up like this for several days at a time. It's good to keep a bird book on hand to be able to identify new ones when they appear. Clearly, the great spring migration is on.

Charlotte Lukes

Purple Finch

Grosbeak Antics

Cardinals, which are members of the grosbeak family, Fringillidae, were not known to nest in my hometown of Kewaunee, when I was a boy. It wasn't until I got into the army, at Fort Sill, Oklahoma that I saw my first one. That was in the early 1950s. And, it was the bird's sprightly "cheer, cheer, cheer" call that first attracted me. I was doubly delighted to discover that such an unusually beautiful call could be matched by an equally striking visual impression.

After my service hitch, when I began teaching in Madison, I added the rose-breasted grosbeak and the evening grosbeak to my life list. Little did I realize that the day would come when I would see all three of these "gross beaked" beauties at one instant.

The rose-breasted grosbeaks had been coming to my feeders for about a week this spring, and the cardinals—as permanent residents—rarely missed a day all year. It was the evening grosbeak that surprised me by completing the trio.

Ordinarily, during years when evening grosbeaks winter in our area, they depart for their northern nesting sites by mid or late April. Hard telling what made the difference this year. Perhaps the sunflower seeds were especially good. At any rate, the unexpected appearance of the evening grosbeak provided me with what will very likely be a once-in-a-lifetime experience.

A rose-breasted grosbeak presented me with a similarly memorable happening. It occurred while I was teaching in Wisconsin Rapids. The spring migration was in process, and just the day before I had told my classes what to do with a bird that had hit a window and knocked itself unconscious. I had advised them to put the bird into a large paper bag, squeeze the top shut, and leave it there for a while. If the bird came to, they would soon know about it.

On that day, one of my students brought in a beautiful male rose-breasted grosbeak that she had helped in just this way, but the bird did not look as though it would pull through. In fact, it was so groggy and dazed that it quietly sat in the bottom of an open shoe box and slowly turned from side to side. Nevertheless, it did offer a perfect opportunity for all the members of my science classes to see a live and beautiful bird face to face. Chances are that not a single student has ever forgotten the experience.

After school was out for the day, the principal came into the room to see what he had been hearing about. He stood admiring the bird, and, with a twinkle in his eye, turned to me and asked, "Does he bite?" At the same instant, he presented his finger to the seemingly inert bundle of feathers. WHAMMO! I have never seen a grosbeak latch onto a person's finger as this one did. And I have never seen a more surprised principal. (The bird made him say teacher!)

Needless to say, the poor guy wasn't very happy about the experience. But I was, mainly because it meant that the bird was well and ready to be released. I took the shoe box, still containing the bird, back to my desk near the windows, opened them all from the bottom, and just waited. In a few minutes, the grosbeak hopped out onto the desk, then up to the back of my chair. There he sat for a minute or two. Suddenly, with one sweep, he was out the nearest window and gone. What a day it had been for him, and for us.

Backyard Paradise

It is spring, and every day is filled with drama—some great, some small. I can observe much of it from my kitchen window.

On a recent day, a young rose-breasted grosbeak with soft brown secondaries and outer tail feathers, and a deep pink throat patch about the size of a quarter, was chased away from the feeder by an adult male and female of the same species. I suppose the adults were higher in the pecking order. Seconds later, however, I saw a cardinal feeding there all by himself! Perhaps the cardinal, being a permanent resident here, rates even higher.

* * *

A lone mourning dove lightly waltzes around a chipmunk under the feeder while searching for supper. He side-steps a bossy jay, then settles down to the business of meticulously combing the long grass, overdue for cutting, searching out bits of cracked corn. Several years ago, while doing winter banding, I captured some mourning doves in a mist net and learned that they possess remarkable strength. What interested me even more, however, was their feet. Their toes were entirely missing—perhaps from frostbite or disease; all that remained were clubby stubs on which they hobbled. But they were surviving.

* * *

I enjoy watching the red-winged blackbird come bombing into the top upright branch of the small quaking aspen tree outside the kitchen window. He hits it at a goodly rate of speed, then snaps back and forth several times in a beautiful, springy, swinglike action. If one could look back into the past few hundred generations of this bird, one would probably find that it lived to a great extent among vertical plants such as the cattails. Examine the feet and toes of a redwing and you will discover they have an extremely strong viselike action. The back claw, especially, is formed to enable the bird to clamp onto or dig into these upright plants with a fierce grip. More than one redwing has sunk his hind claw, long and sharp, into my fingers while being banded.

*   *   *

Rose-breasted grosbeaks do not back up for blue jays! Indeed, they fairly bristle when a jay lands near them in the aspen tree.

The two-inch plus rainfall the other night, accompanied by lightning, provided the plants with moisture and released nitrogen to such a great extent that many plants (including grass and dandelions) have shown phenomenal growth within only a 24-hour period. The small aspen now sports leaves nearly long-stemmed enough to quake in the breeze.

*   *   *

The chickadee that has just buzzed in for supper wears a band so shiny that I am sure the bird is one I banded last weekend. And it got the last word in, you can be sure about that. Chickadees scrap the entire time they are being removed from the mist net. They aim their sharp beaks with great accuracy and strike with force at tender fingertips and knuckles, making you say all sorts of things!

*   *   *

A male rufous-sided towhee has just appeared from the tag alders, scratching vigorously among the kindling wood chips next to the woodshed. His shyness usually keeps him away from the pushy jays gorging themselves with cracked corn from the ground nearby. Mr. Towhee sang his ''drink-your-tea-ee-ee-ee'' song over and over this morning in the soft misty rain. Listen for his song in brushy areas and along the edges of woods. The beauty of the melody will open your heart to the towhee. And once you learn his song you will never forget it, nor want to go a single spring or summer without hearing it.

*   *   *

Seeing the towhee reminds me of my first encounter with one when I was a boy. Dozens of spring migrating birds were stopping daily in my folks' backyard. One quiet morning, I heard an unusually loud leaf-scratching commotion down in the old rock garden. Approaching cautiously I discovered for the first time in my life a towhee, busy as could be, scratching and tossing aside and to the rear the dried leaves in search of food. Later, back in the house, I turned to Roger Tory Peterson's *A Field Guide to the Birds* to learn more about this handsome visitor and, rather unbelievingly, I read: "Often detected by noisy rummaging among dead leaves." Golly, did my faith in Roger Tory Peterson zoom!

*   *   *

The tag alder swamp I write of so frequently has come of its own. It survived the harsh, demanding boreal winter and has now burst forth with spring greenery. Unfortunately it also eliminates one dimension from my kitchen window observations. I can, with ease, see a hundred or more feet into the swamp during the leafless months of winter. Then I spy on the dancing of the grouse, the preening of the goshawk, or the hammering of the pileated woodpecker. But the solid bank of leaves now hides this from me. From now on, well into October, the fierce little six-legged denizens of the wetlands, the mosquitoes, will add an entirely different dimension to those who cannot live without the marvels of the wet lowland areas. Summer, here we come!

Patch Of Sky

"Sweet-sweet, where-where, here-here, see-it, see-it, sweet-sweet, where-where, here-here, see it, see it." A small sprite of a bird—that sad little, glad little, mad little bird—was twisting us around its little feather. Somewhere high amid the green leaves of a maple tree, a dazzling indigo bunting sang its heart out, thoroughly frustrating a large group of bird-watchers.

Finally, as though tiring of its hide-and-seek game, this ultramarine blue braggart flew to where it seemed to be happiest—the highest tip of a bare branch. There it continued to sing, announcing to the whole countryside, its inhabitants, and its early morning visitors, that it was the most beautiful solid blue bird for miles around.

This male bunting's shy, retiring, drab brown mate was hidden from view, perhaps incubating eggs in a nest concealed in the bushy growth of ferns or weeds. Few other birds confuse as many birders as she does, for few are as nondescript.

The song of the indigo bunting is easy to identify. Sung usually in phrases of two, the notes are different-pitched and tend to become weaker at the end. In upper Michigan, near the northern limits of the bunting's breeding range, the number of summer daylight hours is greater than in our area. There, these radiant repetitious singers are known to sing from 4 A.M. to 8 P.M. One counter who studied the vocal accomplishments of this amazing creature estimated that one male might sing his rollicking melody as many as 263,000 times in a period of 61 days!

Look—as well as listen—for this bird along the edges of woodland clearings, where roads border wooded areas, and where there is brushy ground cover. Remember that the males like to sing from high perches, including electric wires and TV antennas.

The other morning the first bunting we heard and located was perched high in a dead tree between the sun and us. One of the hikers said, "How can that be an indigo bunting? It's black, not blue!"

She was right. It was black. However, if the bird had been to the west of where we stood, the early morning light to our backs, that male would have appeared to be a sparkling, luminous rainbow blue. The reason I say ''appeared'' is that the bunting has no blue pigment in its feathers. The same is true for the bluebird and blue jay. Instead, individual feather cells refract or bend the reflected light from the bird to our eyes so as to cause him to appear blue. When backlighted he is dark gray or black.

Farmers and orchardists should welcome buntings to their land, for these birds include in their diets weed seeds and scores of harmful insects, including grasshoppers, beetles, and caterpillars.

Whenever I see a male indigo, glowing blue in color, I'm reminded of one of my favorite semi-precious stones, *lapis lazuli*. In fact, the bunting has a western cousin called the lazuli bunting. That bird also sports an eye-catching amount of azure blue on his back. Painted buntings of the south show a rich blue only on their heads.

Make a beeline to bunting country, indigo that is. Learn its song and discover its favorite perches. Then you can enjoy its sprightly, colorful concert for the remainder of the summer, for he even sings into early September. Welcome this tiny patch of sky with the heavenly voice into your life. You won't regret it.

Soaring Swallows

One of the friendliest groups of birds, and perhaps the least offensive by some people's standards, are the swallows. Any animals that devour as many insects as the swallows do are bound to be looked upon as beneficial.

The first tree swallows I was ever shown were really nesting in trees—actually the tall stump remains of trees that had been drowned and were now surrounded by water. It was a perfect environment for both the insects and their predators, the tree swallows.

The glistening, irridescent blue-black backs and pure white undersides of the tree swallows easily set them apart from all other swallows in this area. These hardy birds are the first swallows to migrate into the region each spring. As hole-nesters, they compete with other hole-nesters, such as bluebirds, house sparrows, starlings, and woodpeckers, for living space.

Their tiny size was impressed upon me once when I was examining some of my bluebird nest boxes. I raised one of the hinged roofs and was surprised to see a tree swallow on her nest. She remained motionless as I looked at her from within 12 inches. How large the box appeared with that tiny bird inside!

When I was a boy, hundreds of bank swallows nested in the steep clay bank along the shore of Lake Michigan, south of Kewaunee. These birds have brownish backs, off-white breasts, and a thin brown band across the lower throat area.

Both the male and female bank swallow help to construct their long tunnel-like nest cavity, which can be as much as 60 inches deep. Depending upon the nature of the material, they can tunnel up to 3 or 4 inches per day.

The first year I taught in Algoma, I learned of a large colony that lived in the clay bank at the city dump, south along the lakeshore. When I arrived to band some of the swallows, I received a very unwelcome reception from the caretaker. He didn't want anything to happen to "his" birds because they helped to hold down the insect population at the dump! A thorough explanation was required before he allowed me to band several hundred of the birds.

The next year, before I had a chance to continue my banding at the dump, I received a sad phone call from the caretaker. Animals had dug dozens of gaping holes into the nest cavities and had destroyed nearly the entire colony. Upon seeing the sorry sight the following day, my first guess was that badgers had been the predators. Cats, skunks, and minks are also known to prey upon these birds, their eggs, and their young.

Certainly one of the most graceful and maneuverable birds in America is the barn swallow. This bird with the deeply forked tail is also a true friend to the farmer. Unfortunately, modern farming does not appear to provide nest sites as did the old-fashioned open-door type of farming. But if you would like to have some barn swallows for tenants, here's a suggestion on how to make them welcome. Nail a couple of 2 x 4's, their flat sides horizontal, against a building about six inches under the eaves. Barn swallows, as well as cliff swallows, will readily accept these sites for nest building.

Several years ago we observed more than 2,000 cliff swallow nests constructed on the sides of two barns on a farm near Deerfield, Wisconsin. This was said to be the largest colony of its kind in the world. The farmer had nailed many dozens of long 2 x 4's onto the sides of his barns. In addition to this he aided the birds' nest construction by creating huge mud puddles in his yard. Sadly, however, each year it seems that house sparrows take over more and more of the intricately shaped gourdlike mud nests that the cliff swallows have laboriously constructed.

Look for rough-winged swallows along the rocky cliffs bordering shorelines. Cave Point County Park, in Door County, is an excellent place to observe them. You can recognize these birds by their dusky throats and light undersides.

Perhaps the best known of all swallows are those from San Juan Capistrano in southern California. It is said that these cliff swallows will return every spring on March 19 to the San Juan Capistrano Mission. So famous is this legend that it became the subject of a popular song.

One surely should include the purple martin in the swallow tribe. Few birds in America have received as much publicity in recent years as these marvelous devourers of insects. Griggsville, Illinois, claims to be the purple martin capital of the world. If everybody throughout our country would give as much attention to many species of birds and their welfare as Griggsville does to its martins, what great improvements in living conditions would be seen, for people as well as for birds!

Bird Of Many Voices

It is morning. Our neighbor's rooster welcomes the rising sun. A couple of bluejays perched on the Koenig feeders hammer away at sunflower seeds while one male red-winged blackbird scrutinizes the ground below for whatever crumbs might have fallen.

A wood thrush hidden somewhere in the tall spruces sings a song of such contrasting beauty to that of the rooster that one wonders how they can both be birds. All these sounds are pleasant to the ear, yet none captures my attention quicker than the whirring sound of the hummingbird's wing beats as she hovers at "her" feeder, containing red-colored sugar water, within three feet from where I sit.

As I listen to these sounds, I think of a question I frequently ask young children as we study birds. "Supposing you had the privilege of naming this bird, what would you call it?"

This challenge is especially fun outdoors, where the students can both see and hear birds they do not know. Imagine, for example, a shy gray bird that slinks in the trees and shrubs nearby calling forth with a meowing sound several times a minute. It doesn't take the children long to visualize a winged cat in gray feathers—the catbird.

Some people in the South have named this mimic the black mockingbird. Obviously it plays second fiddle, at best, to the true mockingbird!

If you listen carefully to the catbird you will discover that it is, indeed, an excellent mimic and that it sings with great charm. But when it came to naming this well-groomed bird, its catcall won out.

Some friends and I stood on the long footbridge between the range-lights the other day, watching several birds. The two that elicited the most interest were a northern waterthrush and a catbird. The waterthrush, tiptoeing and teetering over fallen branches and trees near the water in search of food, is a common sight in the area. But a catbird pursuing aquatic insects in and near the water was an unaccustomed visitor.

121

Perhaps this was the one I banded a few days ago while a group of students watched. They had marveled at its spunkiness and its repeated squeeky calls of protest as I placed the band on its right leg. Yet when handling a catbird, one gets the impression that it is a rather delicate creature. Another thing that surprised the students was the bird's flashy, rusty-colored under-tail coverts.

Responding to a catbird's mimic song, one person imagined the bird singing in Chinese. Rarely does this bird, in its rapid-fire lingo, repeat a phrase twice. Like mockingbirds they will include non-bird sounds in their repertoire, such as squeeky doors and church bells.

The catbirds' secretive nature confines them to dense tangles of shrubs, vines, and the thick plant growth surrounding swamps and ponds. Areas such as these are also perfect sources of food. A little less than half of what they eat consists of insects; the remainder includes fruit such as mountain ash, poison ivy, elderberries, black alder, sumac, wild blackberries, and bittersweet. If you want to distract catbirds' attention from your favorite strawberry patch or cherry tree, plant several Russian mulberry bushes nearby. Studies have shown that they favor this fruit over all others.

If you can get close to a catbird, you might be able to observe its pugnacity. First, locate its nest. Then, using either a bird "squeeker" or firmly kissing the back of your hand, imitate the distress calls of nestling birds. Immediately, and with unbelievable vigor and persistence, this gray scrapper, with its shrieking catcalls, will attempt to drive you away from its nest.

Catbirds are an outstanding "community" bird and are among the first to respond to the distress calls of other birds. Perhaps a screech owl will have to be driven out of the neighborhood, or maybe a snake has eaten one too many nestlings and needs to be evicted from the area.

Welcome back for the summer, gray singer, mocker of cats, friend of man, and champion troubleshooter of the bird world.

Hukweem–The Loon

Three and a quarter inches of rain fell yesterday, answering the hopes of farmers and gardeners. We watched the birds come in to feed as the rain intermittently drizzled, sprinkled, and poured. The birds appear to know exactly how long their oiled feathers can hold out the rain and when it is time to head for cover.

One bird, the loon, which we observed last Saturday morning, has superior waterproofing. Its plumage, unusual for a bird, is firm and compact, perfectly suited for the diving and underwater swimming he does.

Our first sighting of the loon occurred just before we paused on the Kangaroo Lake causeway to watch the bobbing flight of the black terns as they hunted for food nearby. Suddenly, the unmistakable silhouette of another bird, as it flew toward the shallow, reedy north end of the lake, riveted our attention. Its rapid wing beat, along with its downward reaching neck, gave it a hunchbacked appearance, and its large webbed feet trailed along behind as it flew. All these features identified it as a common loon, a rare sight in Door County.

I wish I were able to describe its song in such a way that you could experience the same thrill I did when first I heard it. What a symbol of northern lake-country music! At times the long, mournful wailing call can fool you into thinking a wolf is doing the vocalizing. It is a plaintive, tremulous pleading, frequently sounded while the loon is reared up on its tail. The echoes and re-echoes produced by loons on small tree-surrounded lakes give us one of nature's most beautiful sounds. And their zany laugh-like call has given rise to the expression, ''crazy as a loon.'' Once you hear this bird's song, I am sure that you will never forget it.

It is possible that an old Scandinavian word, ''loom,'' meaning a lummox or awkward person, was used to describe this bird years ago. For sad but true, the grace and beauty it possesses under water is completely lost on land. Its short legs are set so far back on its body that the loon becomes a helpless creature if it accidentally alights on land that is too far removed from water.

Once in the water, of course, it's a different story. Few birds in the world can match the underwater prowess of this skillful swimmer. Much of that prowess results from powerful muscles that control the birds' upper legs, which are located, in part, within their bodies.

Loons can remain under water for more than two minutes and can swim to great depths. Fishermen have caught them in their nets at points as deep as 200 feet.

Loons have the ability to pull their feathers tightly in toward their bodies, expelling much of the air trapped in them. When they do this, they sink slowly, quietly, and ripple-free beneath the surface of the water. Their bones, like those of the grebes and unlike those of most other birds, are solid.

Loons have an extremely high tolerance for carbon dioxide. Their oxygen requirements for long deep dives are fulfilled not so much from the free air in their lungs, as from the oxyhemoglobin and oxymyoglobin that are stored in their muscles. The dark flesh of most diving waterfowl reflects the presence of both of these vital substances.

In order to become airborne, loons must run for considerable distances on the surface of the water. Because they have more body weight per square inch of wing than nearly all other flying birds, they must also take advantage of existing winds.

This remarkable 8- to 10-pound, 36-inch-long bird enjoys a lengthy life. Records of banded loons have shown that some have lived in the wild to be 23 years old.

Britishers call loons the great northern divers, and most other Europeans refer to them as black-throated divers. Years ago, Indians of our region gave this expert diver the name "Hukweem." Most lakes all across northern North America into Greenland and Iceland have at least one breeding pair.

Unfortunately loons have a low survival rate. Many fall victim to waste oil given off by ships. Frequently only one of the offspring will survive and be reared by the parents. But then how the elders guard this tiny buoyant black ball of feathers!

For many years, loons were considered detrimental to the fishing industry and, as a result, many were shot. But studies have since shown that their diet also includes water plants, insects, crayfish, and various mollusks.

We long for the day or night this summer when we will hear the beautiful, wild, haunting song of the loon on one of the nearby lakes. Surely this music will carry with it a touch of wilderness that all of us need in our lives.

The Nightjar

Last night was a whippoorwill night. At least the solo voice of the concert, like a broken record, called this well-loved phrase over and over. It all began as we left our friends' home, first pausing outdoors in the still moist evening to listen to the sounds of the dark.

As a chorus of gray tree frogs trumpeted their shrill notes from the pond in the hardwoods, there occurred a vocal duel between two whippoorwills. First one, then the other called. Soon, both were calling together. How clearly one could detect the slight difference in pitch and variation of their songs.

My awareness of the songs merged into subconscious thoughts of the birds as I slept. But it wasn't long before a whippoorwill near our backyard jarred us into conscious recognition of his presence once again. Over and over and over came the call, reminding me that there is good reason for one of this bird's common names—nightjar! From that moment onward my sleep was turned on and off, on and off, by this persistent singer until the neighbor's rooster launched into his regular 4:30 A.M. recital.

I wasn't in the mood to count the "loudmouth" whippoorwill's repetitions, but it probably ran into the dozens, or even hundreds. For a long time John Burroughs, the famous naturalist and writer, claimed the hearing-record of more than a thousand consecutive calls by one bird. Several years ago, August Derleth established a new record of consecutive whipoorwill calls by counting in excess of 1,100!

Whippoorwills and their relatives, the hummingbirds and swifts, all belong to the same general group. Their main similarity is their relatively long, strong wings and weak feet. It is a rare occasion indeed to see any of these birds—with the exception of a hummingbird—perching on a branch as does a cardinal or a sparrow.

An old European legend, dating at least back to Aristotle, blamed whippoorwills for stealing milk from goats' udders. Following this, the story continues, the udders dried up and the goats became blind.

Hence, another of their names, "goatsucker." In fact, their family name, Caprimulgidae, literally means, to milk a goat. The species name, *vociferus*, meaning noisy or clamorous, seems particularly apt.

I accompanied a group of boys on a campout to a wooded river valley northwest of Madison, a part of the Wisconsin River system. Whippoorwills seemed to be everywhere in those woods. We made a game of sneaking as close to the calling birds as we could before they would fly away into the faint dusky sky. The closest we came was about 15 feet. Two things amazed us—the loud, ringing clarity of their songs and their exceedingly silent flight as they winged to another spot nearby to resume the songfest.

It appeared that those birds had never read the stories written about them nor the scientific descriptions of them in bird manuals, because they didn't say "whip-poor-will" at all. Their call sounded more like "cuck-RHIP-peerior-REE, cuck-RHIP-peerior-REE, cuck-RHIP-peerior-REE," with accent given to the "RHIP" and "REE" sounds. All of their songs were sung while the birds were at rest, never while in flight as is more typical of their cousins, the nighthawks.

What superb, dull, speckled camouflage the whippoorwills have. These creatures, slightly larger than robins, bear a perfect combination of gray, brown, buff, and black, making them practically disappear from sight into the floor of the forest. Try as we might, we failed to spot one whippoorwill during the daylight hours of our campout.

However, luck was with us on one of our early morning bird hikes a few years ago. We sighted a whippoorwill as it rested lengthwise on a tree-shaded old fence rail at the north edge of a woods within 30 feet of the road. Its huge eyes of the darkness were now reduced by its eyelids to narrow slits. My spotting scope brought the bird into what appeared to be only a few feet from our group as we observed this once-in-a-lifetime spectacle.

The whippoorwill lays its two eggs on the forest floor. It builds no nest other than the natural depression which forms from incubating the eggs day after day. The newly hatched young have down on their bodies but need close attention and warmth from the parents.

Their food is caught entirely on the wing at night or during twilight hours. Bristles at the corners of their wide gaping beaks increase their insect-catching effectiveness.

In winter these fascinating birds roam as far south as Costa Rica. Their close relative, the poor-will of the western United States, actually

127

hibernates during the winter in rocky crevices, its body temperature lowered from 102 degrees F. to about 65 degrees F. Breathing decreases considerably and its digestive processes stop completely.

Few prevalent birds can compare in elusiveness with the incredible whippoorwill, which is seldom if ever seen by most people, yet is frequently heard by those who live in or near the country. This mysterious creature of the dark hours, whose ghostly wandering voice sings a song that is its complete character, will continue to be as welcome a part of our night as the robin is of our day. Surely the whippoorwill shall remain the premier summer singer of the nighttime woods.

Wolf-whistler

Every so often someone asks me, ''Of all the birds, which is your favorite?'' It would be easier if they had asked me, instead, which bird I like best in January, February, the first week in June, the second week in September, etc. It also would be much easier choosing a favorite of the wild grassy meadow, the cedar swamp, or the sedge meadow. Something deep inside tells me to be cautious about singling out one creature as being better than all the others.

I will admit, though, that in June, the open rolling pasturelands of this area harbor one of the most exciting of all birds. It's about 12 inches long; it has long legs, knobby knees, a slender body, a thin neck, and a small head; and it likes to perch on the tops of posts. It is so tame that it often allows a person to approach to within 75 or 100 feet of where it stands, nervously chattering and eyeing its greatest enemy, man. It could, indeed, serve as a symbol of gentleness. Following nesting, its strong wings and great strength will carry it 7,000 to 8,000 miles from its breeding grounds, which lie as far north as southern Alaska, to its wintering areas in the pampas of Argentina. The bird, of course, is the upland plover, recently renamed by the experts as the upland sandpiper.

Colloquial names applied to birds by people who have never had access to a bird book have always appealed to me. These people, frequently farmers or other outdoor people, live close to the animals and observe them carefully. Perhaps the bird's song appealed to them, hence the name quaily. Or maybe the bird's habitat will give it its name, such as uplander, prairie pigeon, pasture plover, or prairie snipe.

Stuffy ornithologists occasionally call this bird by its Latin name, *Bartramian* sandpiper, after John Bartram, the naturalist. In keeping with the suggestion of the American Ornithological Union (AOU), we'll call it the upland sandpiper. It really is a sandpiper rather than a plover, even though one rarely sees it near shores and mud flats, the common locales for other species of sandpipers.

129

It probably was the gradual reduction and eventual extinction of passenger pigeons, which were in great demand by greedy gourmets, that caused the increased hunter-interest in upland sandpipers. These tame, trusting, magnificent creatures were slaughtered by the hundreds of thousands just to please the pot-bellied epicureans. Fortunately, several leading and respected conservationists, including Dr. T. S. Roberts, of Minnesota, voiced their concerns that the upland sandpiper was nearing extinction and needed protection. And just as fortunate, the right people in government listened and were persuaded to take action. If the same campaign could be waged in the pampas region of southeastern Argentina, where these birds are still shot by the thousands for food, perhaps they could once again increase in numbers.

I would like to see the upland sandpiper population increase for two reasons. The first and most important reason is usually overlooked or disregarded: This bird is of great benefit to farmers in that it helps to control insect pests. But what seems to be happening is that each year more and more pesticides are used in the fields, thus killing a major food supply for upland sandpipers and other birds. Coupled with that insult is the steady destruction of the bird's habitats.

The second reason I want to see this sandpiper thrive is one of mere aesthetics: It is beautiful to look at and a pleasure to hear sing.

Last Tuesday, while my partner, Mike Madden, and I were taking the annual breeding bird survey, we counted 46 of these noble and talkative birds. On our 30th stop, along Gardner Road in southern Door County, we were thrilled to count 18 of them, breaking a record that dates back to 1966.

By studying the various sighting records of these birds throughout North and South America, I estimate that they spend about 5-½ months in Argentina, 2-½ months on their migratory routes, and 4 months on their breeding grounds in the United States, their principal summer sanctuary.

Several years ago, in late June, two friends and I were returning home from gull banding on Spider Island when we spotted an adult upland sandpiper running across the road, followed by several downy chicks. We were on County Trunk ZZ just west of Appleport. Even though we got out of the car immediately and searched diligently, we failed to find even one young bird. The next day the same thing happened. But this time we got down on our hands and knees and found the young birds crouched low to the ground within six inches of the

Charlotte Lukes

Upland Sandpiper

edge of the blacktop. We merely wanted to look at them, but mama put up quite a fuss out in the mowed hayfield and was found and followed in seconds by her young ones.

Last Wednesday, our group of 15 birders encountered a sandpiper that was a regular "ham." Perhaps a nearby nest or the presence of some young chicks was the cause of its nervous disposition. Whatever the reason, the bird perched on a fence post along Summach Road and repeatedly gave its very rapid scolding "QUIP-ip-ip-ip-ip" call, said as fast as you can say the words. Each time it called, it flicked its tail, eyeing us warily and untrustingly all the while. Our binoculars and spotting scope brought the bird into breathtaking closeness and clearness. The 6:30 A.M. sun sidelighted it with soft and radiant beauty, a thrill beyond my powers of description. Several nearby bobolinks provided background music. And three other upland sandpipers displayed their strong soaring flight, circling high above our heads, then returning to the ground in a rather steep swift dive, fluttering very sandpiper-like with their low wing beats, just before landing.

An especially delightful sight occurred the instant the birds landed, for at that moment their wings were lifted high above their heads as though they were trying to touch wing tips. Then, gracefully and slow-motion-like, they folded them to their sides. Now and then one of the birds let loose with what I call their wolf-whistle, consisting of a medium-pitched sweet, mellow, ascending gurgle followed by a long, smooth, drawn out and descending "WHEE-ee-ee-e-e-e-ou-ou-ou."

We observed as many as three young sandpipers running along and across the road, watched very nervously by one or both adults. At one point, the adult took off suddenly, causing a great distraction in the air. We understood the reason for this behavior when we noticed a harrier flying directly over the young chicks that were hiding in the tall grass. Apparently the adult was drawing the hawk's attention away from the offspring.

Early the next morning, I discovered that the birds would not perform nearly as well for me alone as they had for the group of 15 birders. Perhaps the winged actors of the meadows perform best for a larger audience!

Regardless of the conditions under which you see these stately "tattlers," the more you observe them and listen to their ethereal music, the more you will respect and love them. Little wonder this extraordinary bird IS my "summer" favorite!

Boreal Forest King Of Song

Two winters ago, during a period of sub-zero temperatures, I experienced almost daily sightings of kinglets and brown creepers searching for food along the road, fearlessly defying the icy grip of the frequent blizzards that assaulted us. For such tiny, almost weightless bundles of feathers to be able to survive where man, in one moment of carelessness, could quickly perish, is a marvel to contemplate.

Most ornithologists record these birds as being winter residents here in Door County. They fly far north in the spring, to their breeding grounds in the boreal forests. Friendly and amazingly trustworthy, the ruby-crowned kinglets seldom speak in more than high, wheezy, whisper-like notes.

Little wonder then that we were delighted when one of these birds decided to take up residence in the Sanctuary. All summer long it offered visitors a musical greeting that defied description.

Having spent 14 summers in the Ridges, I have come to recognize the songs of the forty-some nesting birds within its boundaries. But last week, as I sat on the porch of the lower rangelight, I heard a song that stumped me. It was quite musical, rich in sound, loud and persistent; and it was absolutely new to me. I figured it had to be coming from a sizable bird, perhaps one of the large warblers. Curiosity soon gave way to a feeling of challenge. It was unthinkable to be hearing such a loud song and not be able to spot the performer.

My wife and I searched the grove of large spruces the next day for nearly a half hour before we finally got a fleeting glimpse of the tiny nondescript bird. That glimpse prompted us to narrow down our possibilities to either an orange-crowned warbler or a pine warbler. Unfortunately, when we listened to the recorded songs of both, we realized that they were but a "drop-in-the bucket" in quality and beauty compared to the song we had heard at the Ridges' entrance.

Two bird-watchers were waiting for me the next morning at 5:30 A.M., listening in awe to this same fantastic song-greeting. I had

132

brought along my field tape recorder and parabolic reflector, hoping to capture this unbelievable song. I was determined to identify the mysterious soloist. The bird continued to fill the cold morning air with music as I recorded its intricate notes. Just to be sure I was getting on tape what I hoped for, I played back several of the phrases, all the while looking down at the recorder.

Suddenly one of the bird-watchers shouted, ''Look! Right in front of you!'' And there he was, not more than four feet away from where I knelt on the ground. His conspicuous white eye ring, olive-gray back, and diminutive size were positive identifiers—he was a male ruby-crowned kinglet.

As fast as I played his song, just so quickly did he answer—indignantly. Then he ruffled his crown feathers revealing a brilliant scarlet-crimson crown patch that was usually concealed. UNBELIEVABLE! It was just extraordinary that this small bird should have so big a song. But he convinced us, over and over, that what he lacked in size he made up for a thousand times over with song.

And not only did this little guy sing while perching, he also sang while flitting about after insects and even while flying. He was perpetual motion with continuous and energetic song, for his tail jerked and bobbed while he sang, as though we were pumping each note out of his throat.

Ka-zee, ka-zee, tse-tse-tse, tew-tew-tew-toodle-oodle-oodle, eedle-eedle-dee-dee-dee-dee, ker-DEE-dee, ker-DEE-dee, ker-DEE, dee.

The first ''ka-zee'' phrase is high, thin, and lispy. It is followed by a lower, musically rich ''tew-tew'' sound that quickly speeds up in tempo and, at the same time, rises in pitch. Suddenly the song jumps an octave and goes into a fast rattle-like ''dee-dee-dee'' song; then, just as abruptly, it drops back down and melts into a beautiful series of rich rollicking triplets, the second note of the triplet being the loudest and the third note nearly a perfect musical sixth above the first.

Kinglet, we admire you more than ever before. You are king of all song in the boreal forest. Stay with us this summer and return year after year. From now on, early summers will not be complete without your marvelous concert. And we promise to take good care of your concert hall, too!

"Fee-bee"

One of the most common bird songs heard year-round in the woods is usually credited to the wrong bird. During many of the bird hikes I lead, it is not uncommon to hear a high, piercing, two-note phrase. When we stop to listen, the singer is almost always hidden from view. ''DEEE-dee, DEEE-dee.''

After everyone has had a chance to hear the almost humanlike whistle, I ask which bird they think produced the beautiful tones. The response, perhaps 99 times out of a 100, is the phoebe. But despite the fact that the bird seems to be perhaps saying something that sounds like ''Fee-bee,'' the singer is not a phoebe.

Imagine the general surprise when I tell everyone that the song is actually coming from a black-capped chickadee! Invariably a couple of people frown slightly in obvious disagreement and say, ''Golly, I've always thought that was a phoebe.'' But it's easy, using simple deduction, to clear up this confusion. I ask, ''Haven't you heard this call in winter as well?'' And they realize that the phoebe, a flycatcher that couldn't possibly survive in the north woods in sub-zero weather, could not be the singer they've been listening to.

A phoebe's song is lower in pitch, airy or almost buzzy or raspy in quality, and less drawn out and musical than the chickadee's. The first sound of its rapid and distinct two-syllable call is slightly higher in pitch and also louder. 'FEEE-be,'' or even ''WHEE-bee'' would be a reasonable phonetic rendition of it.

Recently, my friend Augie Hoffmann called to say that a pair of phoebes was nesting on the ventilator fan located beneath the overhang of his roof. Although these birds are widespread enough to be familiar to quite a few people, they are still sufficiently uncommon to be considered a precious resident wherever they nest.

Augie and I went into the hardwoods next to his house to watch the phoebes' activity. True to their fashion, the birds accepted our somewhat distant presence quite trustingly and went about their business of catching insects on the wing. Often they darted out to capture their prey, then returned to the very twig or branch where they had been perching, their tails bobbing and flicking all the while.

I suggested to Augie that he erect a natural perch about 14 feet from the back window of his home and directly opposite and below the nest. The next day Augie called saying that the phoebes took to the perch immediately and that they were in open sunlight between 9:30 and 10 in the morning. When I arrived with my telephoto lens, the birds carried on as though I didn't even exist, although I did hide behind some cardboard, and I was able to snap one picture after another.

We usually see our first phoebe of the year by April 10. Melting snow produces many little ponds bordered by trees and shrubs, where they can prey upon the first insects of the season. Though insects—largely bees, wasps, and ants—make up most of their diet, they rely upon wild fruits such as sumac, poison ivy berries, blueberry, cherry, and elderberry, when insects are difficult or impossible to find.

Phoebes are often found around old bridges. Here they will build their nests, constructing them of mud, tiny roots, moss, and lichens. Apparently this agile flycatcher demands that his nest have overhead protection from the weather.

I had a pleasant experience with phoebes in 1966, the first year I came to live in the old lighthouse. There was much painting and repair work to be done every day after I finished my work in the Sanctuary. But a pair of phoebes had beat me to housekeeping by a couple of weeks.

The young couple had built their nest on a ledge beneath the overhang of the front porch. Whenever I needed a little rest from my scraping or sanding, I sat next to the front screen door and watched them; their nest was about eight feet from where I sat. Once their young had hatched, I could lure the adults to the nest within seconds by kissing the back of my hand, thereby imitating the alarm or begging calls of the babies.

The most perfect phoebe nest I ever found was built on a tiny two-inch ledge along the cliff of a beautiful remote ravine leading to a natural waterfall at Wyalusing State Park. This secluded paradise impressed me so much that I took my wife to see it on our honeymoon! Much to my joy the phoebe nest was built again on the same ledge. Here was a natural example of how these gentle birds had nested for centuries—before they came to depend upon man-made structures such as bridges and tumbledown, deserted buildings.

For several years I could predict with 100 percent accuracy where we would see a phoebe during our bird hikes. One spot was the old log house at Beaver Valley, where Wallace Grange and his wife had lived in the mid 1930s. The building was now open to the elements. All the windows were broken and even the doors were missing. A stream nearby provided a constant supply of insects in summer and a large patch of sumacs, most of them dead, served as perfect perches from which the phoebes could sally forth into the air after their prey. The sad day arrived, however, when we came to watch the phoebes perform, only to discover that the cabin had been torn down. Naturally the birds were forced to find another nesting site, and hundreds of birders were robbed of their annual acquaintance with the eastern phoebe, one of the classiest birds on the wing.

A Flycatcher Family

It frequently happens that some of the most valuable standing trees in the natural undisturbed woods are the dead ones. Just follow the daily activities of certain birds and you'll discover why this is so. Nuthatches, chickadees, woodpeckers, wrens, some owls, kestrels, and crested flycatchers depend largely upon nesting cavities found in dead or dying trees for their housing. Remove the standing dead trees in your woods and you've destroyed the high-rise apartments of many wild animals.

We received a phone call the other day from friends who live in the woods along the bluff on the west side of the peninsula. They had been walking along their road, when they saw a bird in a tree quite a distance from them. At first they thought it might be a female rose-breasted grosbeak. Then they noticed its rather prominent head and figured it could be a female cardinal. Finally, they got close enough to identify it as a crested flycatcher. It was then that they saw it enter its nesting cavity in a large dead branch stub of an old beech tree.

During the next few days, we observed the nest and were able to see the young and follow the family's feeding habits. Our friends' car, normally parked near the tree along the road, was all but disregarded by the parent birds and, therefore, served as a blind from which to take photographs.

The calls of the fearless, rusty-tailed great-crested flycatchers sounded with authority through the warm, humid maple-beech-hemlock climax woods as we set up our camera. We used the partly raised car window and a special clamp as a sturdy support.

The birds appeared nervous and uncertain upon first returning to the old beech after we had mounted the camera. They made several passes close to the nest hole before they finally adjusted to our presence and brought food to their young.

The flycatchers used two holes to enter and leave the nesting cavity. The upper and larger one was a knothole where, sometime in the past, a branch had broken off the tree. The lower entrance appeared to have been made by a woodpecker, probably in a previous year. Crested flycatchers have a habit of nesting in old, abandoned nest cavities.

My friend Chuck Miller and I noted that each parent made three or four feeding visits during a 15- or 20-minute period, then was away for about 10 or 15 minutes. Once, about 2:40 P.M., both parents were away for a slightly longer period of time, and we could not hear their calls.

Their noisy return always resounded with loud and far-reaching ''whEEP, whEEP, whEEP'' calls. As far as we could tell, the crested flycatchers made this challenging call with their beaks closed, whether they were carrying food or not. The closer they got to the nest hole, the louder were the calls from the babies, sounding surprisingly like the adults, but not nearly so shrill and commanding.

We marveled at the delicate plumage of the adults. Soft shades of olive showed in the head and back, light yellow was visible on the belly, and there was gray on the throat and upper chest. Their tails and primary wing feathers were a bright rust and showed beautifully as the birds wheeled and turned while flying to and from the nest. Occasionally, when entering the top hole, the birds appeared to move directly downward showing their yellow under-tail coverts as well as their flashy reddish-brown tail.

Twice, as we sat quietly waiting for action, an adult landed in the elderberry shrub not more than 10 feet from us, saw its reflection in the car's windshield, and flew straight toward us as though challenging that third flycatcher.

The calls of three other birds could be heard nearby—a robin, a blue jay, and a white-breasted nuthatch—but none of them gave even the slightest disturbance to the flycatchers during the two hours we observed them.

We plan to watch the development of this beautiful family of flycatchers until the young have fledged and left the nest. Then, using a ladder, we will carefully inspect the nest to see whether or not that proverbial snake skin is included in the nest materials. Many ornithologists have speculated that the snake skin might be placed in the nest to ward off predators. I tend to believe that it might be simple random behavior on the part of the flycatcher—that there doesn't have to be a reason for this occasional phenomenon, as many nests of this species are known to lack snake skins, and others have been found to contain bits of waxed paper, cellophane, or even aluminum foil.

Those of you who own woodland can do several things to help encourage the survival of crested flycatchers. In the first place, don't try to get your woods to look like a city park. Allow plenty of dead trees to remain standing. Setting out larger-holed nest boxes will help the bigger birds. Too many people only make small, bluebird-sized birdhouses. Furthermore, few people think of placing bird boxes in the woods. You can learn more about attracting birds and setting up birdhouses from the many books available in your library. Get busy before the fall. Don't wait until spring to set up the houses. A number of birds need them for winter warmth as well as for summer nesting. If I owned a woods that didn't have at least one pair of nesting great-crested flycatchers, I would surely do something about it!

We're For The Birds!

The first young rose-breasted grosbeaks of the season are out in the speckled alders begging for attention and food. Their call is a rather quiet but firm, single tone ''weeee.'' Apparently this species, judging by those at the feeders and those seen on our bird hikes, is up in number this year. Conditions for nesting and food gathering have been good.

Such has not been the case for the eastern bluebirds. Their total population in this region, based on reports by bird banders and other observers, is down from that of last year. Even though our June and early July sightings have been quite satisfying, I prefer to rely upon a more extensive nest box, bluebird banding study, such as that being conducted by Vincent Bauldry, of Green Bay.

Within the past 20 or more years, several things have contributed to the great reduction of eastern bluebirds. Increased use of pesticides; severe winters and springs; greater competition from starlings, house wrens, house sparrows, and tree swallows; the clearing of fence row trees, shrubs, and old orchards—all have contributed to the problem.

Mr. Bauldry began his bluebird project in 1955 with an aim toward gathering useful data, improving his knowledge of these and other birds, and helping the bluebird population as much as possible. One challenge has always interested him, that of producing a nest box that would closely resemble the old rotten fence post, a successful and proven bluebird nesting site.

Mr. Bauldry finally hit on a plan which, through repeated trial and research, has proven to be very successful. The nest box he built is 4 inches square and about 14 inches deep. The bottom of the entrance hole is placed 3 inches from the underside of the roof (7½ by 8 inches). Several shallow horizontal saw-cuts are spaced about an inch apart under the hole on the inside front panel. This provides the birds with toeholds for getting out of the box.

The entrance hole measures 1½ inches in diameter and is built up

140

Eastern Bluebird

with a piece of 2 by 4 so that the hole is also about 3 inches deep. This prevents intrusion by aggressive starlings.

Eleven inches from the bottom of the box to the bottom of the hole may seem like an excessive distance. Actually this distance is important for two reasons. The three-inch depth of the hole coupled with the depth of the nest box prevents raccoons from reaching in to destroy the eggs or young. Secondly, the young birds have to be a bit stronger to leave the box, ensuring them a better chance for survival in their new world.

A three-and-one-half-inch diameter hole is made in the top to help prevent house sparrows from trying to nest there. This is covered, from the outside, with quarter-inch mesh hardware cloth. A quarter-inch drain hole is put in the bottom panel of the nest box. House sparrows build a deep bulky nest, then tunnel into it from the side. Rain falling into Mr. Bauldry's nest box saturates the nest and prevents the sparrows from successfully raising their young.

If you are building one of these nest boxes, make the back panel four or five inches longer than the front panel so you can fasten it to a wooden fence post. It is a good idea to clean the house between the first and second broods. The easiest way to allow for removing the old nesting material is to construct the box so that one of the side panels swings out and up.

Mr. Bauldry has discovered that bluebirds tend to favor areas near staghorn sumac. It may be that the fruit of these plants provides early spring emergency food. A majority of our bluebird sightings have occurred in the vicinity of sumac, therefore tending to support this belief.

The Wisconsin Society for Ornithology (WSO) has appointed Mr. Bauldry as chairman of the Nest Box Project designed to learn more about ways of helping hole-nesting birds. About 1,100 people belong to the WSO, an incorporated, independent, research-oriented organization geared to gathering useful data about birds. It is the belief of this group that the more one understands the lives of birds, the more one can help them.

Country "Tyrant"

It seems incongruous to picture a group of birds behaving as tyrants, characteristically acting aggressively—even brutally—and seeming to be unrestrained by law or reason. Yet the more one studies birds the more one realizes that the flycatchers fit this description well. Indeed, it was with good reason that this bird was given the generic name *Tyrannus*.

If you want a demonstration of this kind of avian aggressiveness, here's an experiment you can try. Drive to a lonely country road where there is little automobile traffic. Locate an eastern kingbird and follow its course of activities carefully until you discover its nest. Now approach the nest while making a loud squeaking noise by kissing the back of your hand. You just might end up with a bird or two in your hair! For this daringly defiant and fearless feathered ''dive bomber'' will come at you immediately and will not give up until it has driven you away, downright ousted you, and maybe even scared the stew out of you.

Most people prefer to watch eastern kingbirds from a distance. And, indeed, if you are a safe distance from the bird's nest you should have nothing to fear.

If a crow or even a large hawk should fly into the kingbird's domain, it will soon become clear who is potentate of the place. It is the mighty kingbird. And talk about tenacity. There is an incident on record of a kingbird that was seen ferociously pursuing a low-flying airplane with intentions of driving it away from its backyard! Natives of our area claim that it was not uncommon some years ago to see the kingbird give chase to our national bird, the bald eagle.

If the kingbird is new to you, just be on the lookout for a robin-sized bird that appears to be suited for a formal occasion, tuxedo and all. Its regal black-and-white splendor fits its character perfectly. An unmistakable field mark is the white band along the tip of its tail. How upright and statuesque this monarch perches, head held proudly erect.

The first time I had an uninterrupted opportunity to observe the antics of the "King of Them All" was when I was working during the summer months at a pea viner station west of Kewaunee. The job I had was monotonous "bullwork," and I welcomed the sight of a bird nearby. An old unused hay loader stood rusting within 30 feet of where I loaded the trucks with the boxes of peas. The kingbird perched on the top of the old hayloader and repeatedly swooped out in pursuit of flying insects. It would scan the surrounding air, head turning this way and that, then suddenly launch itself upward on very short rapid wing beats, almost helicopter-like at times. Unerringly it would snatch an insect and then usually return to its favorite perch, the hayloader.

"Mr. King's" voice can hardly be mistaken for any other bird's call. Most often it is a very sharp, rapid, screechy rattle-like sound. The only bird call I know of that in any way resembles the kingbird's is that of the belted kingfisher.

What a thrill it is during the early summer to spot the season's first kingbird. Because it is almost entirely dependent upon flying insects, it times its northerly flight to the availability of food, much as do the swallows.

One of the extreme pleasures of studying nature is to see the unusual, the unexpected, the unbelievable rarity. I have had the good fortune of having such experiences a number of times, and one of them was the sighting of an albino kingbird, ermine-white save for the lower part of his tail, which showed just enough black to set off the neat white band at the tip. And beady black eyes! It was an unforgettable sight as it graced the colorful summer meadow, flitting from fence to mullein stalk, then back to fence post in the characteristic kingbird fashion. With its rapid, quivering wing beat, it appeared to be flying on its very wing tips.

And as though to say, "You've seen me once and that's enough," it disappeared just that quickly. Perhaps that was best. Too much of a special thing might tend to diminish its specialness and leave us dissatisfied with the ordinary but very great beauty of the natural wonders that regularly surround us.

Island Colony Nesters

One of the most valuable birds of our coastlines is usually given a name that does not fit him at all—sea gull. Rarely are these soaring creatures found far out at sea. In fact, the only time I ever observed them at a point out of sight of land was during a boat ride across Lake Superior from Isle Royale National Park to Houghton, Michigan. All passengers had been given box lunches but few were eating them. Instead they threw their sandwiches, bit by bit, to the herring gulls that gracefully balanced above the stern updraft. Seldom did those lazy birds flap their wings as they followed the old Ranger II all the way across Lake Superior, a distance of about 70 miles.

Two of the 16 species of gulls that breed in North America nest each summer in Door County. They are the herring and the ring-billed. Hundreds of them form huge social colonies, especially on the secluded, more protected islands such as Jack, Hat, Hog, Spider, and Gravel. Herring gulls outnumber the ring-billed on the islands along the bayside of the peninsula, while the reverse is true of the lakeside rookeries.

One of the most beautiful of the gulls, seen here only during migration, is the Bonaparte's gull. The striking black head of this classy, gregarious bird makes for easy identification.

If it were not for the keen-eyed scavenger gulls, the harbors and coastlines of our state would be strewn with garbage and dead fish. The size of the wintering flocks of gulls here is in direct proportion to the success of commercial fishing. It is most likely that the huge flocks of gulls that follow in the wake of the farmers plows are benefiting local agriculture both by eating thousands of harmful grubs and by fertilizing the soil with their droppings. The statue in Salt Lake City, Utah commemorating the gulls (California gulls) serves as a reminder of just how valuable these majestic birds are to man.

The herring gull is the most widespread gull in America. The adult herring gull is the commonly seen white-bodied and gray-mantled soaring or perching gull of the coastal regions. Its legs and feet are pink, and the lower mandible of its beak bears a reddish spot. In contrast, the bill of the slightly smaller ring-billed gull has a black ring through both mandibles, and its feet are yellow.

Gulls do not breed until they are adults. This occurs in the third year of the herring gull's life. First-year birds have black beaks and dark feathers. Second-year herring gulls have lighter beaks and legs but still retain many brown feathers and a dark tail.

Immature ring-billed gulls, those born within the year, have much lighter bodies than young herring gulls and also have a neat black band on the tip of the tail.

There is a high rate of mortality among young gulls. In fact, only about 20 percent of all gull eggs result in chicks that will achieve the ability to fly. And many of that number will not survive due to predators and starvation, for the young are abandoned at about six weeks of age and must fend for themselves.

I never thought that gulls would make me homesick. But one day, while we were having gunnery practice at Fort Sill, Oklahoma, a flock of beautiful black-headed Franklin's gulls—birds of the prairies—flew over the artillery range. And, oh, how I longed to be home in Kewaunee, hiking along the shores I loved so much, and watching the screaming and soaring herring gulls.

Two gull experiences that stand out in my memory both took place at Isle Royale National Park, located in northern Lake Superior. An old veteran fisherman, Peter Edison, had his fishing camp on the south side of Rock Harbor, across from the Daisy Farm campground where I stayed. Two fellow campers who had a motorboat invited me along one day for a ride to visit Mr. Edison and to buy some fresh lake trout.

The hardy Edison and his wife had fished from the rugged island for many summers. Their winters were spent in Two Harbors, Minnesota. Peter, whose operations were small and very tidy, had just finished the daily task of cleaning his catch and told us, "Come along with me to dump these entrails by the shore. I'll show you my pet sea gull."

Mr. Edison carried two five-gallon pails of fish remains as we hiked a couple of hundred yards along the beach. Finally, he set the pails down and began calling. Within minutes an adult herring gull flew over and landed smack-dab on top of Peter's head. It was with great

145

regret that I realized I did not have my camera with me. The gull patiently waited on the old fisherman's head until he dumped the entrails onto the beach. Minutes later many of his fellow gulls joined Peter's pet for a gutsy banquet.

In the days following that unusual experience I noticed Mr. Edison out on the bay tending his nets with his pet gull peacefully perched on the bow of the little open boat.

One of the gulls on the docks at Daisy Farm was clearly the boss of all the others. I called him Joe, the Harbormaster. Frequently he would perch on the roof of my Adirondack shelter patiently waiting for a handout. I could easily discern him from the other gulls by a knobby growth on the inside of one of his legs.

One day, near the end of my stay, I was cooking my breakfast over the fire and needed some water for coffee. Unfortunately, I forgot all about the three-inch slab of bacon lying on a pan near the fire. When I returned, I found Joe perched contentedly on top of the shelter devouring the last of my precious bacon. As angry as I was, I had learned the hard way that here was one ''gull-darn'' smart bird that was capable of bringing home the bacon!

The "Sugarholic"

Since early June, Charlotte and I have been entertained by a squirt of a bird that measures just a little more than three inches in length—a female ruby-throated hummingbird. Part of our pleasure comes from watching her drink sugar water. Indeed, we think she is a "sugarholic" with a great capacity for food.

Recently she amazed us by emptying the feeder (we are convinced she was the only one using it), which holds four ounces of food, in two and one-half days. By my calculations she emptied the glass bottle feeder in approximately 40 hours by actual feeding.

Here is what is so amazing. Her total body weight is about nine-hundredths of one ounce! This means that she was removing her own weight in liquid food every hour. One is almost forced to presume that she had been feeding some of this to the young in her nest. Whether this is true or not, we don't know. But if it is true, it is a complete mystery as to how she does it.

Sometimes, just for the fun of it, we count the bubbles that rise in the glass bottle as our dainty friend removes the sweetened liquid. A five-bubble drink is a big one! Her long tongue, tubular at the tip, darts in and out rapidly all the while she is feeding.

Our friends, Ray and Louise Hotz, called several days ago with the exciting news that they had discovered a ruby-throated hummingbird's nest in an arborvitae tree in their front yard. The nest—a beautifully constructed, walnut-sized nursery made entirely by the female—was about 20 feet above the ground, and two white eggs, 12.9 by 8.8 millimeters, had been laid in it. The mother will incubate them for about 19 days before they hatch. After birth, the young remain in the nest for up to 25 days before leaving to develop their own food-finding skills.

The sparkly, dark-eyed mother hummingbird scrutinized me suspiciously even though I tried to appear as unobtrusive as possible while balancing at the top of an eight-foot ladder, taking pictures. Frequently, she perched near the nest and either preened herself or glared at me. Each time she moved one-half inch to one side or the other, she accomplished the movement by flying, rather than hopping!

Once she took off from the nest at what appeared to be top speed, probably around 30 m.p.h., and flew directly across Kangaroo Lake. At first this surprised me, but then I remembered reading that hummingbirds are known to migrate nonstop across the Gulf of Mexico, a distance of 500 miles!

Not once did she flinch as I clicked the shutter. My camera was focused and ready for action the instant she landed. Each time she came onto the nest she sat in the same direction, head facing east, tail toward the west.

Soon my friends will be seeing two tiny beaks above the edge of the nest. Before the young leave the nest, they should be sitting quite high, ready to fly without lessons. As I looked at this tiny nest, a true work of art, it seemed to me that it was about three-eighths of an inch higher than the nest I collected at the end of summer several years ago. That one, the outside partly covered with bits of *Parmelia sulcata* lichens, measured an inch high and one-and-one-half inches wide. A soft-drink bottle cap would cover the opening!

Whenever we watch the ''hummer'' at our feeder, we detect little movement at the wrist and elbow joints of her wings. She hovers in the air, helicopter-style, with her wings in a plane parallel to the ground. High-speed cameras have proven that the wings of this tiny dynamo beat 50 to 70 times per second. Obviously the miniature marvel needs lots of food for energy.

Most people think that hummingbirds rely on nectar for the majority of their food. Actually, they find their daily fat and protein in the form of insects, inside primarily reddish blossoms. They also gather some nectar, frequently transferring pollen at the same time.

Imagine Charlotte's surprise recently as she leaned out of the kitchen window in the process of placing the newly filled hummingbird feeder back on the hook. The female hummer flew directly to the feeder and fed right out of her hand!

The decreasing air temperatures this fall will trigger the hummingbird's southerly migration of as much as 2,000 miles. They will leave us with the same thought they have inspired in previous years; that the most precious, inspiring, fascinating bird in all the eastern United States is the ruby-throated hummingbird.

Birding Thrills

One of the strangest birds ever to enter my life did so several years ago while I was conducting a winter bird census near Kewaunee. We had just finished combing the river bottom climax forest for ruffed grouse and were trudging back to the car through about a foot of snow. The hill was long and steep and, to make matters worse, I was carrying the spotting scope and tripod on my shoulder.

Just about the time the long climb was beginning to "get to us" four birds breezed in from nowhere and alighted in the top of a maple tree less than 50 feet from us. When a bird-watcher can produce a "lifer" unexpectedly, it is quite a thrill. For me, this was such an experience—the birds were red crossbills!

That was the first and last time I saw red crossbills, until just the other day. Reports of crossbills in the area had been reaching us for several weeks. One day, a friend from west of the village invited me to observe a flock that had been coming to his feeders daily.

Talk about tame! At first Charlotte and I parked our car in the driveway and cautiously watched through binoculars. Then we got out of the car and approached the birds for a closer look, only to find that we could reach down and nearly touch them as they fed from the ground.

Crossbills are nomads with a reputation for irregular appearances in the Midwest. They breed in late winter and early spring—rarely in May, June, or July when most other songbirds raise their young.

Males, late in the summer, sport very little red in their plumage. Rather they are quite yellowish-olive in color. The young have streaked plumage. Their wing and tail feathers are edged with pale buff. And the unusual bills of these birds are designed so that they can effortlessly extract seeds from evergreen cones.

Crossbills, like other birds that eat only seeds, relish salt and will return again and again to a salt block. Birds that consume insects as a part of their diet obtain natural salts from their food.

Bird-banding has been very rewarding during the past few weeks. Of particular interest has been our study and close-up photography of birds in the various stages of their post-nuptial molting. Several adult blue jays are just about the most motley looking creatures we have seen at the feeders all summer. They have lost nearly all of their head feathers and, as a result, have a vulture-like appearance. Sometimes a skin condition, spread by mites, can cause this temporary baldness.

The rose-breasted grosbeaks continue to amaze us with their attractive feather changes. The young males are particularly handsome as their rosy throat patches begin to show through the rich buff-colored breast feathers. And the hummingbirds would hold our attention from dawn to dark if only we had the time.

A minimum of three hummers, all apparently females, come to the feeders regularly. Blacky is the boss. Her rather blotchy breast indicates that she is an adult female and is molting. Whitey—tiny and sleek and having a light-colored breast—is perfection on wings. Vicky has been named after the ''V'' pattern of darker feathers that adorns her breast. Of course this is a young bird, and the ''V'' may eventually stand for Victor instead of Vicky!

Last evening after supper, I was delighted to discover in my mist net a female baby cardinal, who, with her two brothers, has been coming to the feeders daily. The males are jaunty, with their red feathers beginning to show. But the female! What a prize she is. What class; what perkiness!

And did she make a fuss when she got caught in the net. She could bite just about as hard as her parents. I hope the pictures we took of her will help to educate and thrill hundreds of school children during the coming year.

It's 5:30 A.M. as I finish writing this. The rooster began his crowing exactly 30 minutes ago. Mr. Cardinal joined the rooster, and outshone him (!), at 5:15. But the big surprise came at 5:30, just a second or two ago. Which bird do you suppose was the first to arrive at the feeders? Blacky, the hummingbird! I watch with great pleasure and think about those people who are still snoring at this hour. If you are among them, give yourself a surprise. Get up early some day. Watch the sky light up in the east, and listen to the wild creatures come awake. I promise you won't be sorry!

The Cherry Birds

I well remember my first sighting of cedar waxwings at Toft's Point because of the surprise involved. Boyhood experiences had taught me that these sleek "masked bandits" were cherry eaters of the first magnitude. Imagine, then, my amazement when I saw them catching insects on the wing, more graceful in their movements than some of the flycatchers that are "pro's" at this activity. They soared upward on strong wings as though entering an aeronautical stall, hovered at precisely the right spot, then effortlessly snatched an insect in mid-air.

The silky looking crested nomads nest in more backyards than most people realize. Perhaps it is their poorly developed voice, their quietness, that helps to conceal them so well. On the other hand their bulky easy-to-see nest enables one to study the rearing of their young.

These gentle birds take their name from tiny, bright red, waxy extensions on the tips of some of their secondary wing feathers. It is thought that these sturdy tips help to protect the feather ends, a possibility that could be of considerable importance for a bird that spends much of its time searching for food in shrubs and trees.

In handling my first cedar waxwing, I discovered that they have very strong bills and relatively short legs. The sexes are much alike. Both have velvety fawn-colored plumage, a white edge on their throats, black masks, and a narrow band of yellow along the tip of the tail. Immature cedar waxwings are less brightly colored than the adults.

One of the nicest features of these birds is that a person never quite knows when to expect them. Their strong graceful flight will sweep them into a winter hedge of highbush cranberries and they'll not leave until every last berry has been devoured. Then you wake up one morning and, gypsy-like, they are gone. Closely knit winter flocks, always appearing sociable and dignified, roam the snow-covered countryside. Seldom, if ever, do they have trouble in locating food.

Several of these lispy-voiced beauties are so fond of the serviceber-

Charlotte
Lukes

Cedar Waxwing

ries that grow along our early morning birding routes that we rarely miss seeing them. Most of the fruit is eaten a week or two before ripening, apparently making no difference whatsoever to these gluttonous rascals. Wild cherries (as well as those commercially grown), red cedar, juniper, dogwood, grape, and other wild fruits rank high on their list of favorite foods. Insects are caught and fed to their nestlings. I once tasted some juniper berries and found it difficult to imagine how these birds could stand to eat them. The fact that they digest their food in from 20 to 40 minutes helps to explain this phenomenon.

Some friends and I had the good fortune to observe the seldom-seen nesting rituals of a pair of cedar waxwings. Tony Kotyza had just finished telling me that the female of the pair was beginning to lay her eggs when I noticed the two birds up in a silver maple tree. One was rapidly fluttering its wings while the other gave it food. My friend had been wrong, or so I thought. Surely this was a parent and a nestling.

Seconds later the bird I had thought was the young flew to its nest in the lilac bush. It had really been the female being fed by her mate. Our guess was that she was experiencing a critical stage of egg laying or incubation and was unable to search for food. Perhaps by behaving as a quivering helpless baby bird, she prompted her mate to feed her. Or maybe he was a brand new groom and she was giving him his first lesson in feeding the young birds that would soon arrive on the scene!

Occasionally a person thinks back on an event in his life and regrets having acted in a thoughtless manner. Such an incident occurred in my life when I was a 12-year-old squirt with a new ''Christmas'' BB gun. The summer after I received the gun, the backyard was loaded with luscious ripening fruit and at least a dozen hungry cedar waxwings. I decided to play the role of the hero. One after another the waxwings fell victim to my pellets. Soon, all were buried in the garden.

It pained me terribly to cover those velvety birds with soggy, wet soil. And to make matters worse, we soon found that what the ''cherry birds'' didn't get the robins, catbirds, and brown thrashers did. That deed left me with a pang of sorrow that I've never forgotten. To this day, although I sympathize with the urges of little boys who own BB guns and also with people who grow cherries, I hope that they don't make the mistake I did. (Fortunately, the majority of the cedar waxwings' food consists of wild fruit.) My feelings of remorse will never disappear, for I believe that cedar waxwings are among our most immaculately groomed and refined birds.

153

"Look Around You!"

Henry David Thoreau, in his journal for August 20, 1851, said, "A traveler who looks at things with an impartial eye may see what the oldest inhabitant has not observed." Oh, how often this point has been made apparent to me.

Just the other day, while leading a tour, I had been explaining the phenomenon of the witch's broom on the white spruce. The day being unusually warm, we ducked down onto a narrow, shady trail that was off the beaten path. It was a favorite spot of mine where the clintonia fruit would be their bluest of blue at this time of the year.

Here, too, we could marvel at the huge excavation made by the pileated woodpeckers in the tall, flat-topped white pine. Having refreshed ourselves, we were preparing to return to the main trail, when a little boy piped up, "Isn't that a big old witch's broom right above your head in the tree you're leaning against?"

Many times in the preceding seven years, I had leaned against that tree without once realizing that here was an excellent teaching specimen with which to complete an important lesson in our boreal forest. I had been too steeped in a routine to open my eyes.

Another rare opportunity stared—absolutely glared—at me for four full years before someone "pushed my nose a little closer." This was the glacial relic, the Iceland moss lichen *(Cetraria islandica)*.

Snuggled against the sand amidst the horizontal juniper, it virtually shouted for attention each time I kneeled down to explain about the growth and beauty of this prostrate evergreen. What had appeared to be some sort of scaly brown dead plant material turned out to be one of the rarest plants in Wisconsin, known to grow only in Door County and near Muscoda.

Dr. John Thomson, the renowned University of Wisconsin lichenologist, pointed it out to a group of us one day by exclaiming to me. "Gee, I'm so surprised to see the great quantity of Iceland moss lichen here, a mighty rare plant in our state!"

And I, silently gritting my teeth and mentally kicking myself in the backside for not knowing it, had to ask, "Oh, really? Which is it?" My ears turned red when I saw the hundreds of obscure little patches of it laughing up at me from where the juniper trailed. Since then I have learned that far to the north of us in the caribou rangeland, the Iceland moss lichen is one of the three or four most important winter foods of the mighty caribou. Indeed, it is also one of the few palatable lichens for man's emergency survival in the tundra. Although it usually appears brown and lifeless, rain or even heavy dew will bring it to life, green and spongy soft like so many tiny narrow leaves of rusty green lettuce. "Let us" not go into this embarrassing story any deeper!

Returning to Thoreau's earlier statement, I'm happy to admit that I was also on the "giving" end of this lesson a number of years ago. It happened on a sunny May Saturday along the Wisconsin River, south of the city of Wisconsin Rapids, where my objective was to observe migratory birds returning to their breeding territories. It so happened that the day was ideal for fishermen, too. A large pondlike lake, dotted with huge acre-sized patches of cattails, lay along the road, as perfect a site for fishermen as for a lone bird-watcher. I tried to be as unobtrusive as possible as I glassed the area with my spotting scope. And as busy as I was eyeing the birds, so too were the old-time fishermen eyeing me suspiciously.

Finally one of them blurted out, "What ya lookin' at?" And very nonchalantly, without turning my head from the scope, I replied "Yellow-headed blackbirds."

He shot back at triple volume, "WHAT?"

And I repeated, this time looking him square in the eye, "Yellow-headed blackbirds."

Somewhat astonished he retorted, "Yellow-headed blackbirds? Do you feel all right? Are you sure you know what you're looking at? I've been fishing here over 25 years and I've never seen one!"

Within a few minutes a dozen or more fishlines had been reeled in, their owners lined up at the scope taking turns looking at the handsome yellow-headed blackbirds out among the cattails. Little did I ever think that a day would come when I would be converting fishermen into bird-watchers! Now, as I look back at these "eye-opening" experiences from both vantage points, the loud and clear message tells how important it is, how easy it can be, and how much fun it is, to "Look around you!"

155

Turned On To Terns

Every year early August signals the arrival in the Baileys Harbor bay area of migrating common terns and Caspian terns. At least a couple dozen of each species linger for much of the month. Apparently, the birds find ideal fishing and resting spots here. Unlike gulls, which can thrive on human garbage, the terns are, in a sense, real thoroughbreds—they demand live food.

Thirty-nine species of terns are distributed throughout the world, with 10 in North America. All are strong and graceful fliers. The common tern and the black tern nest in Door County. In past years, during periods of low water, Caspians have nested on some of the ''reef'' islands off the northeast coast of the county. We usually see Forester's terns as they pass through the area during migration.

Terns are, as a rule, smaller, more slender, and more graceful than gulls. However, the Caspians we are seeing now are about the size of herring gulls. The Arctic tern, which breeds in the far North, migrates to the Antarctic, then returns to the Arctic the following spring, is known for its extraordinary endurance.

One of the most beautiful sights of summer is watching the terns hunt for food along the shallow water near the shore. Flying with light, easy, and bobbing wing beats, they effortlessly patrol the bay. When they sight a fish they suddenly hover, appearing to be quite ecstatic over the find. Then they plunge downward in a streamlined power dive and smack the water with a splash. In about one out of four tries, they surface with a fish.

The ''Kee-keek, Kee-keek'' call of the common terns is a musical treat compared to the raspy, raucous ''squawk'' of the Caspian.

As these jaunty common terns ride the August shore breezes, they sport black caps, white bodies, swallow-like tails that are deeply forked, and blazing orange beaks that are sometimes tipped with black. The common tern can be distinguished from the Forester's tern in that the outer tail feathers on the common are black, and those of the

156

Forester's are white. The birds are similarly marked in all other respects except for their breeding plumage. Then the wing primaries of the Forester's are whitish and the common's are gray.

I remember once as a boy when I ''lucked'' onto a dozen Caspian terns resting on a mud flat along the Kewaunee River. The day was very windy and the birds naturally were all headed into the wind. This tended to magnify the beauty of their black swept-back crests, but it was their long, startlingly bright coral-red bills that caught my eye.

The Caspian's large size is deceiving. Occasionally they soar quite gull-like and ride the waves feeding much as gulls often do. But if one notices the bobbing course the bird is flying, and if one can see how the head is cocked sharply downward much of the time, with the flashy bill pointed toward the water, then it is obvious that the bird is not a gull but a tern.

Black terns can be found in several areas of Door County during the summer, particularly Kangaroo Lake, North Bay, and near the Mink River. The causeway crossing Kangaroo Lake is an ideal spot from which to observe their hunting methods. These sleek dark birds favor marshy areas adjacent to open water. Their food includes such tasty morsels as crayfish, tadpoles, frogs, and minnows.

Banding studies of terns in the Cape Cod and Lake Michigan areas, dating back 30 or more years, have revealed interesting facts about these birds. For instance, more than 20 percent of the adult population dies each year, yet some individuals have lived for as long as 25 years. Most often terns lay only two eggs; occasionally, there may be three, and only rarely four. Sadly, the number of terns is declining, a fact most likely caused by a shortage of food brought about by the deterioration of water quality. In addition, there has been wide-scale destruction of their nesting habitat. But, perhaps most insidious of all has been the effect of DDT spraying for mosquito control. Even though the use of this pesticide is now prohibited, its presence will linger in our waters for many years.

Terns that nest in Door County most likely spend their winters along the coast of the Gulf of Mexico and the west coast of South America. Originally it was thought that they migrated south along the Mississippi River flyway. But banding studies have proven that their migratory flights take them eastward through gaps in the Appalachian Mountains to the Atlantic seacoast, then south to their wintering grounds. The origin of this strange movement probably derives from the time of the last glacier. As the climate warmed and melted the glacier, the Great Lakes first drained to the ocean through the Hudson River, not the St. Lawrence, as it presently does. And so, through many thousands of years the terns from our area have followed the ancient route pioneered by their ancestors.

Break loose from your busy late summer schedule and go out some early morning to watch the terns as they, in their breezy bobbing way, hunt for food. The terns won't mind it a bit and you will thoroughly enjoy these classy creatures. Go ahead, do yourself a good tern!

Rain Crow

The first sound that aroused me this chilly morning, other than Howard Mann's roosters across the way, was the welcome song of a black-billed cuckoo. Kloo-koo-koo-koo; kloo-koo-koo-koo; kloo-koo-koo-koo. Over and over, almost nonstop. It is one of my favorite sounds, and it provided a pleasant accompaniment to the large puffy clouds blown in by the brisk northeasterly Canadian air.

Although cuckoos and their relatives (including the roadrunner of cartoon fame) are quite common throughout much of the world, few people in America know the yellow-billed and the black-billed cuckoos. I vaguely remember hearing the term ''rain crow'' when I was a boy, but I had no idea that this was a widely used colloquial name given to our native cuckoos. Perhaps those who still use the term have rarely, if ever, seen the bird that does the calling. Chances are they would be amazed to learn that this ''crow'' has a white belly!

Experts tell us that the first cuckoos made their way from Eurasia into North America via the Bering Strait. It is the common cuckoo of Europe that possesses the real cuckoo-clock-like call. In fact, it says its name with remarkable clarity. Beethoven beautifully set its call to music and included it in his Sixth Symphony (the Pastoral).

The generic name for cuckoos is *Coccyzus*. This alludes to the similarity of the shape of its bill to that of the coccyx (tailbone) of the human skeleton.

European cuckoos are well-known for their parasitic habits, frequently laying eggs in other birds' nests. Our native cuckoos seldom do that. Biologists are quick to point out that this practice is biologically sound and acceptable in spite of protestations from some human ''moralists.'' In fact, cuckoos are part of a natural community—an ecosystem—that is a complicated and constantly changing combination of biological and physical elements.

To realize how valuable the cuckoo is to man, one needs only to catalog the bird's favorite foods. Among them are tent caterpillars, fall webworms, cankerworms, tussock moths, and many other hairy and spiny caterpillars consumed by very few other animals. One cuckoo's stomach was found to contain 325 fall webworms. (The fall webworm is occasionally quite common in Door County. It covers branches of leaves, whereas the tent caterpillar is more common in spring and is usually found in the crotches of branches.) Some of the cuckoos' stomachs that were examined were found to be completely lined with the furlike hairs of spiny caterpillars. Cuckoos are known to be able to regurgitate this unusual stomach lining.

Frequently, bird-watchers are led to cuckoos by the birds' song, but generally these birds are shy and prefer to remain concealed. It is the black-billed cuckoo, according to human standards, that has the more musical and liquid song which I described earlier. Our yellow-billed friend is harsher and louder, singing a rapid "kuk-kuk-kuk-kuk-kowp, kowp, kowp" (or kloop, kloop, kloop).

Even though the ranges of the two birds overlap, the black-billed cuckoo is considered to be the more northern species. It was a black-billed that provided me with one of my most interesting bird-banding experiences. My mist nets, covering a distance of about 200 feet, had been set out before dawn along a lonely stretch of road that wound its way through a tag alder swamp in Honey Creek Valley. Unfortunately, the birds just were not moving. Time after time I checked the nets, only to find them empty. Finally, as I approached one end of the string of nets, I saw a large jay-size bird hit the net at the far end. I ran to that end quickly, hoping to get there before the bird escaped, but it got away when I was about 20 feet from it. It was a black-billed cuckoo, and I could have kicked myself for not having been able to run faster.

This shy, ghostly recluse perched about 40 feet back in the alders peeking at me from behind leaves and challenging my Bohemian stubbornness. My immediate plan was to slosh through the swamp around and to the rear of the bird in hopes of flushing it back into the net. When I reached a point that I thought was near to and opposite the bird, I shouted and clapped my hands, chugging knee-deep through the muck and water. It was a messy business, but it worked. Huffing and puffing, I ran up onto the road to find my captive cuckoo resting comfortably, lying hammock-like on its back in one fold of the net. Oh did I gloat!

All the way back to my banding station, 100 yards or so away, this red eye-ringed beauty quietly followed my every move. What a beauty!

Fortunately, I was able to take photographs with one hand as I held the bird with the other. When all was done, I joyously and pompously strode back down the road and returned the bird to where I had captured it. There, to my unbelieving eyes, was its mate, or what I took to be its mate, captured in the very same fold of mist net where the first prize was caught! That really made my day!

Perhaps that experience was meant to last a lifetime, for it was the last cuckoo to grace my hands. Nevertheless, the incident intensified my fondness for the species, an affection that grows and grows each year.

I hope that there will always be enough hairy caterpillars to feed these pleasant birds, and I hope that every bird-watcher will be able to experience the joy that comes from hearing the cuckoo's song and watching its swift and easy graceful flight.

Sharpie

Many meat-eating bird-watchers, who never question the conditions under which the animal they eat was killed, will for some strange reason tolerate only vegetarian birds at their feeders. Seed eaters such as chickadees, evening grosbeaks, and cardinals are always welcome; but the sharp-shinned hawk, the Cooper's hawk, and the goshawk remain persona non grata. These people apparently cannot accept the fact that predatory birds do not wantonly kill their songbirds but rather do so only in order to remain alive, just as you or I might eat a plate of roast beef or a chicken dinner.

I mention the three hawks, all accipiters (the Latin word for hawk), because 95 percent, or even more, of their diet consists of other birds ranging in size from small warblers (prey for a sharp-shinned hawk) to a ruffed grouse (easily consumed by a goshawk).

Sharp-shinned hawks have been on my mind ever since yesterday when Charlotte and I visited a friend, Tom Erdman, who traps and bands hawks each fall. In a good year, he bands as many as 600 or more. Tom had already caught three ''sharpies'' by the time we arrived. Even though the low-pressure weather system was bringing unfavorable southerly winds, the overcast sky allowed us to see the hawks approaching from a considerable distance to the north. We hid from view inside the ''hawk hut,'' peering out through long narrow openings at eye level.

Several species of live bait, which Tom is federally licensed to use, were strategically tethered outdoors. These included a pigeon, a dove, a grackle, a starling, and a house sparrow. Different types of nets, some spring fed and triggered to be released from indoors, were set in place. Generally, the aim is to use the large showy white pigeon initially to attract the oncoming hawk. The small hawks are then attracted by the smaller birds into the trapping area where they are harmlessly caught in one of the nets. The lure birds are not harmed.

Meticulous notes are taken on every predaceous bird seen,

whether it is trapped or not. When a hawk is captured, a thorough analysis of its plumage is recorded, measurements are taken, and the bird is weighed before being banded and released. Surprisingly, the female sharpies are considerably larger than the males, with bodies as much as three to four inches longer. One theory is that nature has kept the males smaller so that they will not destroy the female and the young. They are indeed aggressive creatures.

The three accipiters found in this region all have several characteristics in common. Their tails are proportionately long and their wings short and rounded. Their flight pattern consists of several quick wing beats followed by a glide, then more wing beats, and into a glide again.

Adult sharp-shins are a dark blue-gray on their upper parts, with breasts and abdomens barred a dull reddish-brown and white. First-year birds have brown upper parts and whitish breasts and abdomens that are heavily streaked with brown.

These smaller of the accipiters favor the woodlands and their borders for both nesting and migrating. In fact it was along an old logging road near the edge of one of my boyhood woods that a male sharpie put me to a test. I had been photographing bog plants at a small lake southwest of Kewaunee and was on my way back to the car when a loud robin-like chirping attracted my attention.

This fussing, which appeared to be an alarm call, led me down an old road toward some tamaracks. The sound was coming from about 20 feet up in one of the trees. The second I raised my head to search for the nest, the small hawk swooped down to within a few feet of me. I wanted to see how persistent the fierce little creature could be, but on one pass he came too close for comfort.

The episode ended with his becoming so obsessed with chasing me out of his summer domain that I had to cut a willow branch—my flag of truce—and hold it above my head as I scurried out of the woods.

These amazing birds breed from northwestern Alaska south into northern Mexico. Their southerly migration approaches its peak during the latter days of September. An unbelievable record was set by hawk watchers on September 22, 1970 at the Hawk Ridge Nature Reserve in Duluth, Minnesota, when a total of 1,510 sharp-shins were counted on that single day. In the fall of 1970, 69,214 hawks and eagles were tabulated there! Generally, more than 30,000 are seen there during September, the peak migratory month for accipiters.

Sharpen your sights for the southward-bound sharpies. Above all, look often to the sky this fall to drink in the sun, the colors, and the crisp air. Occasionally you'll see the littlest accipiter of them all, the daring marvel of the bird world, the sharp-shinned hawk.

Mockingbird Concert

No creatures in my yard provide me with more pleasure each year than the cardinal. The color of both male and female makes them outstanding in the winter especially. And certainly their songs, come early spring, are second to none. Close study has shown that cardinals nest from April through mid-September. Three broods are common, though four, and even five, have been recorded.

Just this morning, as the eastern sky began to show good light, about 6:15, I saw two cardinal families, each consisting of an adult female and two young. The brilliant pinkish-orange beaks of the adults clearly set them apart from the dark-beaked young ones. A couple of the young begged vigorously for food, squatting rigidly, wings held somewhat away from their bodies and quivering rapidly, their heads held slightly upward, mouths open in anticipation of a sunflower seed. But their begging was pretty much in vain this morning. Indeed, their easy days seem to be over. They are now on their own.

*   *   *

A huge wave of warblers settled in the Sanctuary yesterday, busy feeding on insects in the conifers. There were hundreds of them, mostly those hard-to-identify fall warblers. Mixed in with the crowd were thrushes, kinglets, and some migrating chickadees.

Recently many people have been asking me, ''Where are the birds?'' Or, ''What has happened to all the birds?'' I generally don't say it, but SOUTH would be my best answer. At least that's where some of them have gone, although a lot of birds are still with us. They are different in their habits at this time of year, to be sure, but they are very likely no less abundant than in previous years.

Get out, scratch around a little. Scour the brushy lake banks, creek bottoms, and the edges of the woods. You'll find birds. Lots of them, too. September can be one of the best times of the year to see bluebirds.

Take the off-the-beaten-track side roads. Keep sharp watch on the telephone and fence wires. I bet you'll see more bluebirds in September than you've seen all summer.

*　　*　　*

This past summer was a good one for the mimic birds, the brown thrasher and catbird. Of course the fact that a thrasher had built his nest in my backyard and had his favorite singing perch high up in one of the paper birch trees near my back door made observations easy for me. But I did see and hear others of both species. One of the unusual (rare in Wisconsin) mimics, however, escaped my searching completely this summer—the mockingbird. This vocal star made my list for the past five summers, but not so this year.

The first mockingbird to catch my eye in Door County did so as I traveled west toward Egg Harbor on a June day in 1965. The bird flew from an orchard tree up into a large elm alongside the road. Pure luck, and duck soup to identify; the creature practically told me its name. But that was the last I saw of it that summer.

Well, the following summer, several top bird-watcher friends from Chicago were up visiting, and on Monday (my day off work), I suggested we head toward the middle of the county and look for a mockingbird. As I think back, I remember my friend Karl Bartel asking, rather dryly, "Sure, how many?"

We had been searching for some time when a "possible" darted across the road ahead of us and into the same orchard where I had seen the bird the year before. It was only a robin and my ears turned slightly red. My friends continued to tease: "O.K., where's the mockingbird?" Or, "Some mockingbird!"

To make a long story short, we burned up a lot of gasoline looking for that fictitious animal. As a last desperate resort, I led our two-car caravan slowly past the orchard where I had once been successful (along County Trunk E). When I arrived at the stop sign at County Trunk C, I had still not spotted the bird.

Then, looking into the rearview mirror, I noticed that Karl's car was nowhere in sight. I had been so mockingbird conscious that I never once noticed that he was no longer following me. I was sure he wasn't lost, so I turned the engine off and waited.

About five minutes later, Karl came over the rise, faster than

166

usual. He screeched up behind me, waved an arm out the window, and greeted me with one word: "mockingbird!" They had found it! Margaret Lehman, a passenger in Karl's car, had been listening with the car windows turned down when she heard a suspicious bird call. They had stopped, backed up, and sure enough, there it was, as big as day.

As things turned out, I was glad I had my tape recorder along because that "ham," performed beautifully for us. Its repertoire included both northern and southern birds, such as the chuck-will's-widow and the tufted titmouse. Over and over, this character imitated its relatives, several dozen different species in all. What a concert!

And to make matters even better, the bird remained in its territory most of the summer and sang for many spellbound *homo sapiens*. Here, truly, was an "out-of-stater" we welcomed with open heart. It brought enjoyment that will live for a long time in the form of a taped concert. Thank you, Mr. Mockingbird!

Chicken Of The Woods

We've felt the first broad sweep of 40-degree autumn ''arctic'' air. It has the aspen leaves quaking on their stems. The first hint of yellow on the leaves contrasts beautifully with the crisp blue sky. The mosquitoes have finally been tamed and the blazing colors of the woods, like blaring trumpets, lure people to these resplendent outdoor palaces. This is grouse weather, the season of the year when many people have their first explosive encounter with one of these bantam-size ''chickens of the woods.''

Most ruffed grouse, when interrupted during their feast of fall favorites (such as acorns, beechnuts, black cherries, clover leaves, or wild grapes), will reward the startled intruder with nothing more than the whirring sound of their speedy takeoffs. But once in a great while, one of these dauntless little woodland birds utterly dumbfounds the human race and actually takes a peculiar liking to people. These unexplainable shenanigans, the exact opposite of the bird's more common and extreme wariness, establish an indisputable fact: Ruffed grouse are unpredictable creatures.

Several days ago, Mrs. Al Horskey of northern Door County called to tell us that a perky little daredevil of a chicken-like bird strutted out of the nearby woods and immediately became friends with her. She was not so sure she should trust the bird until I assured her, without actually knowing what kind of bird it was, that she had nothing to fear.

The next day, Mrs. Horskey called again. She was quite excited as she told me, ''You really should get a picture of this bird. Why, it was sitting on my lap this morning!'' That settled it. Charlotte and I headed for the ''Top of the Thumb'' the next afternoon, after I had called Mrs. Horskey and she had assured me she would have the bird performing by the time we arrived.

As we pulled into her driveway, we saw her in the backyard, stooping over slightly, having a talk with the mystery bird. Our guess was correct. It WAS a genuine, wild, but dauntless ruffed grouse! We assembled our camera gear, eased out of the car, and inched our way into the backyard, not sure of just how the remarkable little bird would respond to our presence.

Immediately we began taking pictures from a distance, using medium-range telephoto lenses. But we quickly found ourselves having to back up from the little "ham" in order to get it into proper focus. Time after time, I would be ready to squeeze the shutter when suddenly the grouse would put its head down and run straight for the big eye of the camera. It didn't appear to be defensive or malicious, just curious.

We soon noticed delightfully soft purring and clucking sounds coming from the trusting bird. When the grouse wandered out of sight into the woods, Mrs. Horskey would call, "Here birdie, birdie, birdie." Occasionally, she imitated some of its songs. Within mintues the little "birdie" strutted out, ready for more attention.

Now came a sight she had told us about. Mrs. Horskey sat on the lawn, while the ruffed grouse circled her, picking all the while at bits of clover and dandelions. Suddenly, it jumped up onto her lap!

The next day we were in for another surprise. Our friends Jerry and Karen Willey, who had stopped for a chat, listened to our grouse story and suddenly got very wide-eyed. "That must have been the same bird we stopped to photograph!"

Seems that they had been out when they saw the grouse, stopped, and Karen got out to try to get a picture. Much to her surprise the bird did the exact opposite of what she thought it would do. Instead of running or flying away, it came toward her.

This endearing once-in-a-lifetime wild-bird experience could very easily end in tragedy should the grouse's uncanny affinity for humans lead it head-on to the business end of a hunter's 12-gauge shotgun. All we can do is hope for the best, or perhaps even condition the bird with loud noises to remain in the deep thickets or sheltered swamps.

I never have a ruffed grouse experience without thinking about one of the great animal story classics, "Redruff, the Story of the Don Valley Partridge," which appears in Ernest Thompson Seton's great book, *Wild Animals I Have Known*. I feel that we have added a new chapter to our knowledge of the ruffed grouse. After all, how many times have you had a wild grouse come out of the woods and sit upon your lap? When, indeed, was the last time you had a grouse around the house?

Blue Buccaneers

There is no bird we have observed more closely during all seasons of the year, handled more regularly in our bird-banding operations, developed more descriptive characterizations about and, in general, come to feel we understand better than the blue jay. But one more chapter has just been added to our knowledge of its unusual antics; we have discovered that it loves sourdough pancakes!

For that reason, whenever chef Charlotte makes this breakfast treat, she always manages to have several left over from the meal to share with the blue "buccaneers." She allows the specialty to dry for a half hour, then tears them into quarter-sized pieces and puts them outside on the nearest feeding platform.

This morning when she placed some pancakes outside for the birds, I said, "Let's see how long it takes them to find the treasure." The first freeloaders arrived within 15 seconds. Five more were here within another 10 seconds, to help in the raid! How hilarious those greedy marauders appeared in their attempt to cram just one more precious morsel of pancake into their already filled mouths. All seemed to be a flurry of blue as these whirling dervishes continued without let-up until the platter was "licked clean."

A noted British ornithologist, arriving in this country and seeing his first blue jay, said that he considered this creature to be the most beautiful bird in the world. The same thought went through my mind last winter when I saw my first Stellar's jay.

I was outside the visitors' center at Sunset Crater National Monument northeast of Flagstaff, Arizona. The ranger there appeared surprised at my admiration of the stunning, dark-crested jay. "Oh them," he remarked. "They're regular pests."

Years ago, especially around the beginning of the twentieth century, agricultural experts placed a great deal of emphasis upon establishing the economic importance of most wild creatures. In one study 292 blue jays were killed in various parts of eastern United

Charlotte Lukes

Blue Jay

States, and the contents of their stomachs were carefully analyzed. The remains of songbirds were found in two stomachs, and small birds' egg shells in three. But for the most part, the scientists discovered acorns, beechnuts, corn, and pine seeds, as well as beetles, grasshoppers, and caterpillars.

Despite these findings and after all these years, the general public still labels the impudent jay as a professional nest robber of the first magnitude. Personally, I am convinced that John Audubon's famous "Elephant Portfolio" of bird paintings, which includes a portrait of blue jays stealing eggs from another bird's nest, did much to tarnish the reputation of this fine bird.

After listing the pluses and minuses of the blue jay, I find overwhelmingly that this colorful opportunist is good to have around. It's too bad that we can't ask the deer, grouse, pileated woodpecker, chickadee, or chipmunk how they feel about the jays. I have an idea they would answer in one loud chorus, "FRIEND! Our best watchdog. The blue jay alerts us to the first sign of danger."

One of the luckiest moments in my life occurred on the Saturday afternoon when I walked into a tiny bookstore in Lawton, Oklahoma to look for a bird book and purchased my first copy of Roger Tory Peterson's *A Field Guide to the Birds*. The storeowner, who sensed my interest in birds, began telling me about his pet blue jay. After about a half hour of describing the shenanigans, and especially the bird's fascinating "tea KETTLE tea KETTLE, TEA cup TEA cup" call, the man convinced me to join the National Audubon Society.

He gave me their address and I went right back to my army barracks and wrote a letter. The Society was the first preservation organization I joined (and one of the best) and their journal was the first magazine I subscribed to; I still receive it. And all because of a story about a blue jay—that accused robber of eggs, bully, hog in feathers, raucous loudmouth, and the recipient of just too many other bad names to mention.

The blue jays will always be welcome at our house. They may nest in our yard. They may serve as our early morning alarm clock. And they may continue to share with us Charlotte's famous sourdough pancakes.

171

Horicon Honkers

Our first glimpse of the Horicon marsh last weekend came as we approached this vast sprawling waterfowl paradise from the east, on county Highway H. There, from high atop the Niagara escarpment, we feasted our eyes on this prime wetland bathed in the cool hushed glow of dusk.

I wonder what Mrs. Personius and her husband, Bob, manager of the Horicon National Wildlife Refuge, thought as we stood outside their home for several minutes, eyes and ears alert, mouths agape, fingers pointing skyward, as flock after flock of "honkers" sailed low over our heads toward the marsh. Finally, we recovered from our trancelike state and announced our arrival. Then began one of the most delightful 24-hour periods we have ever spent.

We quickly accustomed ourselves to the night-long booming of the farmers' carbide cannons, intended to scare the geese out of their cornfields. I learned that actually there were no geese in the fields at night; all sought refuge in the marsh. Yet the guns, pointlessly, were allowed to operate throughout the 12 hours of darkness, perhaps echoing the farmers' feelings of frustration over the geese eating their corn during the day.

It is interesting to note the variations in abundance of waterfowl at Horicon. After attempts to drain and farm the marshland failed in 1948, only about 2,000 geese were counted there. By 1971 that figure had risen to more than 200,000! Now, in spite of hunting pressure that harvests about one-quarter of the flock, the total number remains quite stable at around 200,000. This is the Midwest's portion of a nationwide flock totaling approximately two million.

My wife and I retired, thankful for the good weather forecast and anticipating a store of exciting bird experiences the next day. Little did we realize, however, that we would be treated to a 4 A.M. concert of great horned owls, three of them, sitting in the tree right outside our bedroom window. Back and forth the serenade went, with each of the

172

three performers on a distinctly different pitch. We think back to this treasured performance as a good omen that ushered in the grandest of goose days, packed with thrill upon thrill.

Skeins of Canada geese, hundreds of them, warily threaded their way through the hunters rimming the marsh. Because the geese are primarily grazers, they spend much of their day feeding on corn, waste grain, and the young tender shoots of many plants. In 12 hours of alternate feeding and loafing, each goose consumes, on the average, about one-half pound of food. If most of the food was corn, imagine the bill for 200,000 birds consuming something like 50 tons of grain!

Tens of thousand of blackbirds, along with many ducks, blue geese, American bitterns, black-crowned night herons, a single common egret and a muskrat (like large wind-up toys scurrying across the dike road ahead of us) joined the Canada geese in the gala extravaganza. Cameras clicked continuously.

All day long I couldn't help but think of a statement made by Francis H. Kortright in one of my favorites of his books, *Ducks, Geese, and Swans of North America*. "Sagacity, wariness, strength, and fidelity are characteristics of the Canada goose, which collectively are possessed in the same degree by no other bird. The Canada in many respects can serve as a model for man."

Their survival from year to year, despite heavy hunting, reflects their greatness. People, perhaps influenced by the phrases "silly as a goose" or "wild goose chase," would be in for a surprise if they were ever to study the life cycle of these majestic, graceful creatures.

It's appalling to think that these geese are hunted for about eight months of the year. Licensed hunting in southern Illinois and adjacent states lasts into mid-January, and natives of the southern Hudson Bay region will be gunning them upon their return northward in May. Fortunately, the great majority of these birds reach the beautiful remote privacy of their northern Ontario breeding grounds. There they enjoy long periods of daylight, with very few predators present, including man.

As long as people care for the honkers' breeding grounds and provide them with winter refuges, the likelihood of their future abundance remains good. But careful study and much work remains to be done concerning the human relationships that touch upon the birds' welfare. An equitable balance must be struck between thrilled goose watchers and irate farmers. The carrying capacity of their wintering grounds must be carefully determined, too.

Having watched flock after flock sail down the invisible spiral stair-case of crisp autumn air, we already look forward to the jubilant trumpet clangor of next fall's first Canada geese, a performance we don't ever want to miss.

Gray And White Gleaner

If you can imagine cracking something open with a hatchet, then the name of the white-breasted nuthatch will make sense to you. The lone well-groomed male who comes to our feeders many times a day frequently wedges a sunflower seed in a small crevice of tree bark and vigorously ''hatches'' away at the husk in quest of the tasty meat inside. Several well-aimed blows with his seemingly upturned beak eventually break away the covering and reveal the tasty prize inside.

The last time I captured a nuthatch for banding, I was impressed with its strong, short, stocky legs and its especially wide stance. Its proportionately large feet and arched toes enable the bird to walk as effortlessly on a trunk when the bird is upside down and sideways as when it is right side up. Unlike the woodpecker, it does not need to use its tail as a third point of support.

This defier of gravity impresses me as being a fussy, inquisitive gleaner of the first magnitude—always on the move. Its economic importance to man is demonstrated by the fact that it devours scores of insects and their eggs. In addition, it eats acorns, pine seeds, and even a little corn now and then.

The range for these bobtailed climbers extends from southern Canada clear into southern Mexico and includes most of the eastern two-thirds of the United States. Even though we in northeastern Wisconsin consider the white-breasted nuthatches to be permanent residents, as documented by banding studies, some of those birds that live in the extreme northern part of the range are known to migrate south in search of a more dependable supply of winter food. The same habit holds true for their cousins, the red-breasted nuthatches, as well as for black-capped chickadees.

Many birds adapt well enough to be able to exist in various forest types. Not so the white-breasted nuthatches, which are seldom found far from maple-hemlock woods, especially when those woods also contain oak trees.

Look closely at the head of the next white-breasted nuthatch you see. Females tend to have less black on the back of their heads than the males. Surprisingly, the young males resemble their fathers, and females their mothers, soon after they have become completely feathered. If you are lucky enough to have both the white-breasted and red-breasted species in your area, you will find that they are very easy to tell apart. The red-breasted is smaller by at least an inch and has a well-defined black eye-line that the white-breasted lacks.

Recently we watched with interest the caching tactics of the white-breast. The board and batten construction of the old woodshed offered him numerous slots in which to cram bits of suet and sunflower seeds—much more than he was eating. A few days later, I glanced out the window to see a red squirrel inching his way up and down the side of the shed feasting on the nuthatches winter hoard.

Few birds have a more distinctive call than the white-breasted nuthatch. Try as I might, I can't come up with a better phonetic analysis than the often-used "Yank-Yank-Yank." The rather loud nasal sound of the white-breast has a richer quality and carries farther than that of his "oboist" cousin, the red-breasted nuthatch.

Sometime in the future, I hope to lure the white-breasted male to my hand using something like peanuts, walnuts, or pecans as bait. I've heard that they tame quite easily and I know that all I really need is lots of patience.

What I plan to do is quietly stand outdoors, arm outstretched on the platform feeder, hand open and filled with nuts. If you've never tried this, I suggest you do. Once you get the feel of these feather-light sprites sitting on your palm and fearlessly accepting a handout, you'll be hooked forever. And if that lucky bird happens to be a white-breasted nuthatch—three cheers for you!

Observations

Six-tenths of an inch of rain, nearly a downpour at times, fell this afternoon. As I sat at the kitchen table, peaceful and a bit lazy, I almost became hypnotized by the pleasant combination of golden milkweeds swaying nearby and raindrops splashing on the platform feeder. Now and then a chickadee buzzed in to the Koenig feeder, snatched a seed, then raced back to the umbrella-protection of the tag alders.

Suddenly, I blinked. I had to look twice to believe my eyes. There, in the middle of this downpour, was a bedraggled cardinal. And what a sight he was, perched on the raised edge of the platform and calling out about a half dozen of his familiar sharp "chirp" sounds. Each time a call was given, he flicked his tail sharply upward, then lowered it slowly. Apparently he was not aware of the puddle of water below his tail. As a result, whenever he lowered his tail, the end of it dipped into the water. Then, when the next call was made, the tail jerked upward sharply and a neat little trail of water droplets was thrown into the air. It was all too beautiful for words.

*   *   *

Small flocks of American coots (known to us as mud hens when we were learning to hunt ducks) dotted the reedy shores of the bays this morning. I remember how we were taught to pass them up in order to conserve precious and expensive ammunition. But these omnivorous lobe-toed members of the rail tribe did fool us more than once into thinking they were ducks. I often wonder if they, along with a lot of hunters, don't realize they're not ducks.

I never tire of watching their splashy takeoff, wings and feet flailing the air and water for some distance. Perhaps their numbers are increasing due to the fact they are scorned by the majority of duck hunters. And yet, to the "good" ducks they generally provide a signal of available food and safety.

177

In spring, one can approach them relatively closely and see that they are mighty handsome creatures. They are dark slate-gray in color, blacker on the head and neck, tones of olive on the back, with red irises and a whitish beak. Their chicks, hatched in early summer, are an unusual color combination of black and orange. The lowly coots are really quite beautiful and deserve more attention than they get.

*　　*　　*

A cold front moved through our coastal area today, pushing ahead of it the balmy summer-like weather and replacing it with cool brisk winds and a clear sky. Tonight after supper, as I returned from the beach, the moon was already showing over the Point. Enough light remained so that I could easily find Deerlick Trail. As I walked along, the eerie yellow glow of the large-leaf asters caught my attention, resembling large glowing hearts scattered all along the trail at ground level.

More and more flocks of Canada geese are threading their way south along the Lake Michigan coast, impelled by the colder weather and snow coming from the North. Unusually early snowstorms in the West make one think back to the unseasonable and unwelcome wet snow that plastered us during the early part of October last year.

It's the time of year that quickens your pace, makes you pull up your collar and muscle up to the frosty change of weather. I'll be putting a coat of spar varnish on my snowshoes any day now, but to all these cold thoughts one of my friends says: "Don't talk about it."

"Ruffed" Turkey

Several tourists who were visiting the Sanctuary in mid-summer came to the nature center one day with what seemed to be an incredible story. They reported that a young turkey had just attacked them on the trail—and that it did not cease its onslaught until they were driven away!

When I heard the account later that day, it was apparent to me what had happened. An unsuspecting ruffed grouse hen and her chicks had been surprised by these intrepid tourists.

Most likely, the hen, as soon as she saw the intruders, sounded her warning cry while the young immediately hid themselves. Next, she probably puffed out her body feathers, extended her tail feathers in that renowned fan shape, and flew fearlessly at the dangerous humans. Obviously her bluff worked, for she chased them away from her most prized possessions, her downy, defenseless young.

It was on that very same trail, around mid-September, that I saw two adult ruffed grouse, unaware of my presence, as they fought vigorously, threatening each other. Their sparring match consisted of running at each other, then jumping into the air with both feet extended forward, wings flailing rapidly.

Neither appeared to be winning. Perhaps it was just a practice bout, preparatory to the real pre-mating aggressive displays next spring. Or it may have involved a claim to the lush stands of highbush cranberry shrubs nearby. During the cold harsh months of winter the seeds of these plump fruits rank high as an emergency food to balance the bird's diet.

I am sure that many of the people who admired and perhaps photographed wildflowers along the trails during the summer would be very surprised to learn that some of these same plants are used by the grouse as food later in the season. Various parts are consumed including seeds, fleshy fruit, and leaves.

A plant that grows in abundance in these parts, yet one that is least conspicuous and least known to people, produces seeds that are much sought after by the ruffed grouse. That plant is the tiny cow wheat (*Melampyrum lineare*). Jewelweed seeds and black cherries rank as two other favorites. Fruit of the bearberry, bunchberry, Canada Mayflower, blackberry, sumac, partridge berry, and sarsaparilla also are included in their primarily vegetarian diet.

In the fall, as much as 90 percent of their food is composed of the leaves of clover, strawberries, dandelions, and aspens. Then the first snows of winter bring about yet another drastic change in the grouse's bill of fare.

When snow conceals the ground-level plants, the grouse moves on to the higher shrubs and trees in search of buds. For about four months, the harshness of winter forces these birds to subsist on a monotonous diet of aspen, birch, willow, ironwood, beech, and maple buds. Apple buds, when they can be found near enough to good cover, provide a rare delicacy. Several years ago, I was almost able to set my watch by the arrival at dusk of several ruffed grouse who must have had a ''sweet tooth'' for the sugar maple buds in my backyard.

The ruffed grouse do much of their winter feeding in early morning or evening, perched in the higher branches and exposed to danger.

There is a high rate of predation upon these hardy birds by the goshawk in areas where the aspen or birch woods contain a few higher perch trees for the keen-eyed accipiter. (Some people think that the word goshawk may be a corruption of the words grouse hawk or goose hawk.)

Ernest Thompson Seton's intensive study of wild grouse prompted him to divide the bird's year into various moons instead of months. January was the stormy moon, February—hungry, March—wakening, April—drumming or pussy willow, May—love, June—chick, July—berry, August—molting, September—gunner, October—acorn, November—mad, and finally December—the snow moon.

Others have described late fall as the crazy season of the grouse, with October being the peak of the period. This might account for the number of phone calls I have received in the past from people who have had one of these powerful little fliers crash through a picture window, seemingly with no reason. Some wildlife biologists believe these erratic flights are nature's way of scattering the brood to prevent inbreeding. Others actually believe the wary creatures are being driven crazy by trying to escape the incessant racket made by falling leaves. These old-timers claim the birds' hysteria decreases considerably after the leaves are off the trees. And there is even another explanation that suggests that the ''crazy'' grouse are those with serious infestations of lice, ticks, or blood-sucking mites.

Experts report that the ruffed grouse is one of the hardiest, non-migratory game birds in this country, even though it must face numerous adversities during its lifetime. Some of those adversities include clearing of land, increasing hunting pressure, severe winters, unfavorable breeding seasons resulting from bad weather or too many predators, scores of body parasites and diseases, and winter invasions by more than the usual number of predatory birds. And as if to add insult to injury, this fine bird, even in his home territory, must listen to tourists refer to him as a TURKEY!

Grasshopper Falcon

The best known of all the predator birds is not much larger than a robin and is native to most of North America. It also is one of the most poorly named—the sparrow hawk. Kestrel is a much more appropriate name for this handsome little bird. Apparently the word is derived from the bird's rattling, kingfisher-like call. ''Killy-killy-killy'' describes it nicely.

We're seeing few kestrels in this region right now because of the absence of grasshoppers in the fields at this time of year. Insects make up as much as three-fourths of the bird's diet, and small mammals comprise the remainder.

Chances are that you were out in the country the last time you saw a kestrel. He was probably perched motionlessly on a telephone wire, patiently waiting for a mouse or a grasshopper to make a move in the field below. And when that move was made, you probably saw the kestrel drop down quickly, capture his prey, return to his perch, and eat it. One of the prettiest sights in all the great outdoors is one of these swift creatures hovering in one spot, treading air, head pointed downward scanning the ground below for its next meal.

The kestrel belongs to the falcon family. Its wings are long and pointed, its tail is long and tapers at the tip somewhat, and its head is rather large. Streamlined would be a good word to describe this bird.

Several years ago, in early fall, I was standing on top of the lake bank north of Kewaunee scanning the lake for gulls, loons, and ducks. A small flock of sparrows was on the ground nearby eating weed seeds and, very likely, leftover grain. Suddenly, just at the exact moment I turned my head to look at the sparrows, a kestrel zoomed into their midst and seized one of the small birds so quickly that the others hardly realized he was there.

Panicked, the flock disappeared in a few seconds over the side of the lake bank, while the kestrel flew to a nearby fence post to devour his victim.

Charlotte Lukes

American Kestrel

The other two falcons native to this area are seldom seen. They are the pigeon hawk (merlin) and the duck hawk (peregrine). In fact, the last peregrine to nest on the bluffs of western Door County probably did so as many as 30 years ago. Their numbers have dwindled to a dangerous low. The merlin, too, is extremely uncommon to this region and is seldom seen.

My wife and I were amazed by the dozens of kestrels we saw perched on telephone wires in central Florida. Before we made a trip across that state, we had not imagined the vastness and openness of this cattle country. It is a perfect wintering place for these birds of prey and an ideal location to count, study, and photograph them.

People can encourage the survival of kestrels by building nest boxes for them. A great majority of natural nesting cavities have been destroyed by landowners who want to citify their property, so down come the old trees with the large holes in their trunks. These are exactly the types of holes needed by these birds.

A crude box measuring 9 to 12 inches square and 15 inches deep will do nicely. An entrance hole of at least 3 inches, round or square, allows for easy entrances and exists. Place some straw, hay, or even coarse wood chips on the bottom of the box and nail it to a tree on the edge of the woods.

And don't settle for one house. Build several. The kestrels will appreciate it and will work at keeping in proper balance those life forms man spends great sums of money trying to destroy.

The Cranes Of Baraboo

Few species of modern-day wildlife are better qualified to serve as the symbol of conservation than the crane. This is the bird that most people confuse with the great blue heron. But one feature, easily observed, distinguishes them—the way their necks are held in flight. The heron's neck is S-shaped; the crane's is outstretched in a straight line.

The first cranes that I chanced to see and hear were in Adams County, north of Friendship, Wisconsin. Few wild sounds thrilled me and my students more than the vibrant, trumpeting, piercing, long-carrying musical rattle of the sandhill cranes. Eventually I visited Wallace Grange's Sandhill Game Farm, now owned by the Wisconsin Department of Natural Resources in southwestern Wood County. There, at close range, I enjoyed Wallace's pet sandhill crane, Silver. What a sharp-eyed inquisitive ''watchdog'' he was! He could very well have been the goodwill ambassador for all sandhill cranes nesting in isolated prairies and fields in the northwestern two-thirds of Wisconsin.

Charlotte and I were recently invited by our friends, the Pavlats, of Madison, to join them on a tour of the International Crane Foundation (ICF), at Baraboo. George Archibald and Ron Sauey, who began this outstanding nonprofit organization in 1972, today have the world's most complete collection of captive cranes. People from throughout the world are helping them in their exciting, worthwhile project. Recently, students from Washington High School, in Germantown, Pennsylvania, raised more than $1,000 for the ICF.

This amazing group of dedicated people could serve as a model for other conservation-minded organizations. The ICF is a registered, publicly supported, nonprofit organization dedicated to the study and conservation of cranes throughout the world. In its organizational charter, the ICF sets forth its five principal goals: (1) Research—to determine the biological attributes and requirements of cranes both in the wild and in captivity; (2) Conservation—to protect cranes and their habitats through the world; (3) Captive Propagation—to establish a species bank of rare cranes within former habitats wherever feasible; and (5) Education—to act as a disseminator of information on cranes to the people of the world.

Tours of the Crane Foundation are welcomed, but only on an appointment basis. They can be scheduled from May 15 until November 15, with Saturdays being the best day. Our introduction to their program came through a slide show presented at a convention of the Wisconsin Society for Ornithology. Our appetites whetted, we had to learn more; hence, our trip to Baraboo.

Terry Quale, ICF's Public Affairs Coordinator at the time, met us at the gate on a cold windy morning. Within minutes she was introducing us to cranes from around the world, ranging in size from the small "demoiselle" to the tall "sarus" cranes of southeast Asia. In fact, it was the sarus who trumpeted our arrival to the entire crane population on the 120-acre farm. Their exotic dance of running, jumping, wing-flapping, and neck-stretching was both comical and beautiful to watch.

The star attraction of the morning was Tex, a female whooping crane. This very tame, noble bird approached to within inches of where we stood, watchful of her unpredictable, strong, stabbing beak. She responded hilariously to Terry's low-voiced call, "Tex, come here Tex," and instantly stretched her neck and gave her piercing call to the sky.

As will happen with domestically reared geese, ducks, and other waterfowl, Tex has imprinted on her master Dave Archibald and now thinks he is her parent. Dave is hoping that Tex will become interested in the Foundation's other whooping crane, Tony, a male, and has done everything imaginable to divert Tex's attention to Tony. I wonder if he has thought of dressing Tony to look like him!

More than half of the surviving 15 species of cranes in the world are endangered. Habitat destruction, especially the drainage of wetlands, is the major cause of the threatened extinction. In discussing this problem, many people raise the worn-out cry, "Who are more important, cranes or people?" I have found it best not to argue with persons of that mentality. However, I am tempted to say in reply that obviously people think they are more important. Look at the many thousands of square miles of concrete and blacktop they have laid on top of fertile farmland. And consider the hundreds of thousands of acres of wetland habitat they have drained. Cranes couldn't do that. It is interesting that *Encyclopedia Britannica* has about six times as much information about mechanical cranes used in construction and drainage projects, than about living, feathered cranes!

Whom will you share your land with? Give me the noble, wary, exuberant, dancing, lively cranes—symbols of a long and happy life!

Northern Scavengers

The other morning, as I trudged through the woods, I heard an almost unbelievable, downright astonishing series of croaks, grunts, bell-like notes, and squeals. Had I not heard these sounds in the past and seen the "singer" responsible for them, I really would have been bewildered. Our northern friends, the ravens, have arrived for the winter—back, black, and welcome! Exactly what attracts them to the big woods I do not know, but whatever it is, I'm glad they're here. They are primarily scavengers, playing the important role of devouring dead animals in the forest.

How deceiving ravens and crows can be from a distance. Both are black, and both have the same general shape. At times, under certain light and atmospheric conditions, a crow can appear unusually large. But seen from 50 yards or closer there can be no mistaking the two. The raven is considerably larger, six inches or more. Ravens have a tendency to soar more than do crows, and their tails are giveaways as to their identity. The raven's tail is diamond-shaped, coming somewhat to a point; the crow's tail is rounded.

It soon became apparent that this small flock of ravens was unaware of my presence. At least that is what I assumed when they continued their hilarious concertizing.

As I stood there, I found myself wondering whether the lower voices belong to the older and larger males and the higher voices to the females. But the sound that really fascinated me, as I knew that a raven was making it, was a low and pure bell-like note. A stranger might bet money that those notes were coming from some source other than a bird.

I leaned up against a tree on this delightfully quiet and pleasant morning, not wanting to miss a single note. Unfortunately, the concert ended abruptly and the ravens began to move about. One bird, apparently not seeing me, flew directly toward me. I was amazed at the noisy flight, especially in light of the fact that I had been discovered.

187

The bird, upon seeing me, speeded up its wing beats, veered off to the right, and vanished quickly from sight.

There must have been at least a dozen ravens calling back and forth on this whisper-still morning. In past winters I had considered myself fortunate to see two at a time. Evidently the large-scale movement of ravens down from the north is directly related to the decrease in the number of hares there, perhaps the primary winter food of this bird.

These shaggy-feathered visitors are skillful, clever, and fearless. Their four-foot wingspan will undoubtedly be seen with some regularity along the shores this winter, right out at the edge of the ice, feeding upon the dead fish. Even though the raven has never been protected by law, it has been able to survive amazingly well through the years. However, man's steady encroachment is forcing these birds to move farther north in search of the undisturbed solitude they seem to require in their lifestyle. (A good many people need this, too, whether they realize it or not!)

Would you believe that a raven in captivity lived to be 69 years old? It's true. They are, indeed, tenacious animals. I am hoping to capture their marvelous vocalizing on tape this November and make it part of our library of wild bird songs.

Make an effort to locate and observe some ravens late this fall and during the winter. They're here and will usually announce their location well in advance of your arrival. Believe me, you are in for a treat!

Worldwide Weaver

Most people would be surprised to learn that a weaver finch is perhaps the most widely distributed and recognized bird in the world. Amazement might multiply when they were informed that about 150 million of these ubiquitous creatures exist in the United States. In fact, you might be looking at one this very instant on the ground beneath your bird feeders. I'm talking about the lowly house sparrow.

I was brought up to call them English sparrows, a name they were probably tagged with because these aggressive little ruffians with short legs and thick beaks were brought to this country from England in 1852 and were released in a New York City cemetery. The only other member of this large Old World family that survives in any number in the United States is the European tree sparrow, which is now common to the St. Louis area.

Birding friends of ours, professors David and Marion Stocking, of Beloit College, joined an early morning bird-watching group while in England several years ago. Naturally they were somewhat uneasy as they went in search of birds they very likely couldn't identify. At one point they sighted a house sparrow and excitedly blurted out, "Oh! An English sparrow!" The Englishman nearest to them gave them an icy cold Jack Benny stare and said, "We don't call them English sparrows here. They're HOUSE SPARROWS!" David and Marion soon learned that the English have no more love for the persistent rascals than Americans do.

House sparrows—a name that should not be taken to give offense to our beautiful North American species of true sparrows—are native to northern Africa, Europe, and western Asia. They thrive with greatest success amid human communities. In addition to being brought here, they were also foolhardily introduced to Australia, New Zealand, Japan, Hawaii, the Philippines, South America, and South Africa.

The Japanese net between five and ten million annually, pluck and clean them, then baste and roast them to be sold for eating as delicacies during certain seasons. Rice-growing countries, in particular, consider these birds to be serious pests.

People dislike house sparrows for several reasons. They steal food from other native birds and frequently take over other birds' nest cavities, particularly those of cliff swallows, purple martins, and bluebirds.

Farmers contend that they are responsible for the spread of chicken, cattle, and hog diseases from one farm to another. Large roosts are both filthy and noisy. A friend once said, ''Oh well, in the city even the voice of a sparrow is comforting.'' But their vocabulary is pretty much limited to a monotonous ''cheep, cheep (cheap!).''

If I must say something complimentary about these hardy little hoodlums, it is that they are good indicators of the environment. Where one has only house sparrows nesting, you can expect to find crowded buildings, pavements, little or no open space, and hardly any trees, shrubs, or grassy areas.

I must admit that there was one time when a male house sparrow thoroughly fooled me. It happened on an early May afternoon in the University of Wisconsin Arboretum, in Madison, when the lilacs and other flowering shrubs and trees were too splendid for words. Suddenly, a bird hopped out from behind some of the plants and I raised my binoculars. Sparkling little creature, black bib, chestnut patch back from the eye, sleek gray cap and strikingly white wing bars—Oh, drat it all, only a miserable, clean house sparrow! Were my ears red with embarrassment. Ordinarily these gregarious scavengers are nothing but dirty, sooty ragamuffins.

How well I remember the thick growth of vines that covered the north side of our home in Kewaunee. And how well I also remember the number of house sparrows that one could, on a warm summer day, chase out of their hiding places simply by throwing a ball against the side of the house. Those were the good old days when our milk was delivered by a milkman driving a horse-drawn wagon. As a result, the streets were littered with horse droppings. And where there were droppings, there were flocks of sparrows, feeding on the undigested oat seeds. A decrease in horses on city streets brought about a similar decrease in the number of house sparrows.

Perhaps one can say something good about house sparrows, for they are known to clean up some of the edible garbage humans leave in their wake. In fact, these birds have done relatively little harm in comparison to native blackbirds, grackles, and, particularly, the alien starlings.

Let us at least be thankful that these social birds, the house sparrows, have a relatively short life span. Consider this mathematical possibility. If all offspring from one pair would live, each reproducing eight young annually, for 16 years, the result would be something like 300,000 million birds! Why, that's three times the world's total bird population!

Phantom Thunderbolt

A small, flicker-sized, feathered thunderbolt—the sharp-shinned hawk—landed unnoticed in the tall hedge of highbush cranberries at dawn in my friend's backyard as we sipped our hot coffee. We were planning our day's bird census and awaiting the arrival of daylight. Suddenly, the accipiter made its move and burst into the midst of a small flock of songbirds feeding at the edge of the shrubs. The "sharpie" made its kill instantly and flew back into the nearby thicket to consume it.

Most birders, especially those who carry on a winter bird-feeding program, become terribly upset if such an episode occurs in their yards. The majority sympathize with the small birds and outrightly condemn the hawk; the tiny bird of prey is labeled a "murderous little villain." And, indeed, many of these energetic and awe-inspriring raptors will be shot by the overly zealous and protective "nature lover" or sportsman, in spite of the fact that all birds of prey are protected by Wisconsin law.

The sharp-shinned hawk, similar to the European sparrow hawk, is undoubtedly the most persecuted of all hawks on this continent. Nesting sharpshins do not hide and cower at the approach of a person. Instead, they viciously defend their eggs or young, thus becoming easy prey for the gunner.

Another factor working against these lightning fast birds is their manner of migration. The most northerly breeding portion of the population is also the most migratory, especially those from Canada and the northern United States. These birds, thousands of them, will migrate in the fall, usually as singles, to Mexico and Central America. They most often fly at treetop elevations or quite close to the ground, constantly on the lookout for prey. Frequently, they surprise uneducated gunners in the field during the hunting season who do not think twice about killing a hawk with a shotgun.

On a single day from one checkpoint, more than a thousand sharp-shinned hawks have been seen during the fall migration season. Two of the best vantage places for such thrilling sights are Hawk Mountain Sanctuary, in Pennsylvania, and the Hawk Ridge Nature Preserve, in Minnesota. The spring migratory habits of these daring little hawks are considerably different. As a result, fewer of them are seen.

We will invariably have at least one or two sharpies in our general area before the winter is over. Apparently there are plenty of small birds around, because the hawks, including the wintering goshawks, have never become pests by making repeated visits to the feeding station.

A pair of sharpshins nested in the Sanctuary, about 100 yards from the observation platform, during the summer. Many visitors described the nervous, high-pitched "dick-dick-dick" calls they heard. A smaller number of us, patient to sit and wait on the platform, eventually got good looks at the "little phantoms." At least that's what they reminded us of as they so silently appeared and disappeared.

Earlier in the summer, my friend Chuck Miller and I were getting ready to begin work on the unfinished observation platform. Chuck was sitting on a small pile of decking stacked approximately four feet from a large pine tree. His back was to the tree as he worked at pulling on his hip boots. I was approaching him, about 40 yards away, when suddenly I saw the sharpie fly toward us from the east in a fast headlong flight. The second it saw me it veered to the right and flew directly between Chuck and the pine tree. It all happened so fast that by the time I hollered to Chuck the hawk was gone. The entire maneuver was so quiet and smooth that my partner had no idea of just what had happened.

I have tried to educate thousands of people as to the essential part the sharpies and other hawks play in the natural economy. But I am sure that many outdoor enthusiasts weaken the second they see one of these speedy accipiters kill one of the songbirds they have been feeding. Bird-watchers are frequently the hardest to convince that the sharpshins are not wanton killers, that it is not malicious brutality which drives them to kill. They simply are HUNGRY!

Sportsmen and birders alike must remember that the cottontails, ruffed grouse, songbirds, and hawks have existed together in wildlife communities in this region for thousands of years prior to the arrival of man. Leave animals and their natural predators alone and none will become overabundant. In fact, if you wish to discover the most dangerous threat to our natural environment, plants, and animals—and the most essential focus for environmental awareness, tolerance, and involvement—simply look into a mirror!

Christmas Bird Tally

Birds, unlike man, quickly adjust to changes in the natural elements rather than fighting them. Imagine four disgruntled birders driving down a rainy country road on December 17, sullen because this was THE day of the year to count birds—the annual, nationwide, "Christmas" bird count. Naturally we were glum, for we realized that the birds' activities would be altered considerably due to the cold, pelting drencher.

As we approached our friend Conde Conroy's place, several dozen birds suddenly flew from the ground up to the wires and maple tree next to the road. I stopped the van immediately and the first word that came out of my mouth was "starlings." But as we raised binoculars to our eyes, we noticed that a few of them were sporting crests.

"Cedar waxwings," I called in a loud whisper. We were out of the car in a second, glasses back up to our eyes, and it was then that I made out the chestnut-colored under-tail coverts as well as the white and yellow wing patches. Now I said in a much louder, exuberant whisper, "Bohemian waxwings!" You can well imagine how quickly my mood changed. These birds had made my day. One by one they settled back to feasting on the crab apples in Conde's front yard.

Ordinarily these sleek haphazard visitors from the West don't travel much farther eastward than the Dakotas. We suspect that a shortage of food in their natural range drives them farther away from their home territory in search of rose hips, cedar and juniper berries, mountain ash, crab apple, and hawthorn fruits.

We had also had a pleasant surprise earlier in the morning while we were out on the Baileys Harbor Point searching for gulls and waterfowl in near gale-force winds. We were just about to leave the spot when Mike Madden saw a bird perched on a power line near the water about 100 yards away. I aimed the spotting scope at the robin-sized bird as it teetered precariously on its windswept lookout, took one look at its telltale black mask, and shouted with glee, "northern shrike"! This hawklike northern Canada nester was obviously scrutinizing the marshy shore for mice and other small rodents, its principal winter food.

Three separate flocks of nomadic pine grosbeaks were the highlight of the morning. One group of about 12, up in the Sand Bay area, was eating the red fruits on a tangle of deadly nightshade, *Solanum dulcamara*. These confirmed wanderers from the north are invariably attracted to red fruits. It is suspected that the rosy red coloring of the males is a dietary product resulting from the red pigment in the bird's food.

Snow buntings down from the high Arctic, common sights during the past few weeks before much of the snow melted, were apparently sitting tight in the open fields, where weed seeds were plentiful. During early December, we had enjoyed watching these gregarious opportunists from the treeless tundra as they scurried over the fields in search of seeds. They would suddenly swirl into the air, looking like a cloud of snowflakes, then, just as quickly, drop back to the ground and resume their feeding, appearing and disappearing with great speed.

We heard evening grosbeaks in every village during our count. Attracted to the people's handouts of sunflower seeds, these high-wheeling "butterflies of winter" start out by entertaining the bird watchers, but end by being accused of eating them out of house and home. They are known for their unpredictable noncyclic, periodic population peaks. Based upon the dozens of reports we have been receiving, this appears to be one of those peak years.

The bay side of the Door Peninsula, in the lee of the storm, proved to be the better of the two shores for observing waterfowl. Common goldeneyes were the most abundant of the wild ducks. One small flock, feeding about 100 yards out from the boat ramp at Ellison Bay, appeared to have a slightly different duck in its midst. It turned out to be another surprise, a white-winged scoter. In all our past 20 Christmas bird counts—begun in 1958—this was the first time we sighted this unusual visitor.

Even though we do not adjust to changes in the natural elements as do the birds and other wildlife, we nevertheless attempt to take some hints from their activities. Frequently, we spend time outdoors hiking, cross-country skiing, working, or studying nature. New sightings and experiences outside naturally lead to indoor research, study, and interesting challenges. The birds, without words, remind us that we should always remain physically active and mentally alert.

Evening Grosbeak (Female)

Charlotte Lukes

Evening Grosbeak (Male)

Feathered Gymnast

If one were to conduct a popularity contest among the wild birds of the forest, attempting to determine the one that is most widely recognized and enjoyed, which do you suppose it would be? My vote would go to a pert, friendly little feathered gymnast, the one the American Indians of this region called "ch'geegee-lokh-sis," the black-capped chickadee.

Residents of Maine and Massachusetts chose this nimble creature as their state bird, and rightly so. The black-capped chickadees live there year-round, as they of course do in other states as well. The northern forest states can by no means lay sole claim to these cheerful acrobats, however. A wide range of environments includes the chickadees—deciduous to coniferous woods, highlands to lowlands, wetlands to drylands.

Their habitat in Europe is limited to swampy lowlands. There they do not have to compete with several other closely related species of titmice, birds that dominate what in North America would be very favorable chickadee country.

These trusting, roly-poly birds reach the peak of their bird-feeder activity in winter. Only an occasional one or two are seen at our summer feeders, while as many as 50 or more chickadees, in addition to other birds, look for a handout on a typical winter day. During a two-day period in the early spring of 1967, I captured a total of 53 chickadees in my mist nets for scientific study and banding.

Imagine my surprise and joy when, in late October of 1973, I recaptured one of the chickadees banded in early 1967. Obviously the bird was hatched during the summer of 1966 or earlier making it seven or more years old. One of the things that most interested me was a definite growth of tiny grayish feathers mixed in with the black head feathers! The record age of a black-capped chickadee, as far as I can determine, is nine years.

Banding, weighing, and measuring nesting chickadees from dif-

197

ferent latitudes has proven that those in the north tend to have larger bodies, giving them less body area in proportion to their weight. This fact helps them to survive in extremely cold temperatures. Another recorded discovery is that the northern birds' beaks, legs, and wings tend to be shorter than those of southern birds. These extremities lose heat more rapidly than the larger parts of the bodies.

And here is yet a third and highly interesting fact: A chickadee's heartbeat speeds up as the surrounding air temperature decreases. An active feeding bird, on a sub-zero day, can be expected to have more than 1,000 heartbeats per minute. Its heart slows down to about 500 beats per minute when it is asleep.

I was quite impressed the first time I removed a chickadee from a mist net. Ed Peartree, of Oconomowoc, was teaching me the art of mist netting. After a couple of weekends of watching him, he finally allowed me to remove my first bird, a chickadee. WOW! What a scrapper! What an initiation! Its body seemed to hum or vibrate in my hand. Little did I realize then what its heartbeat was.

Talk about quickness and maneuverability! Stroboscopic studies of this speed merchant show that it can change its direction of flight in three-hundredths of a second. Its wing beat—about 30 per second—enables it to accomplish this rapid change of direction.

Nearly everyone knows the black cap, white cheeks, black bib, grayish back, and brownish wash of its flanks as field marks of the chickadee. It is generally thought that the sexes are not distinguishable. But, in fact, it may be possible to tell the males from the females because the black cap of the male appears to extend farther onto its back than does that of the female. Also, the male's bib is wider, especially right beneath the beak, and the bottom line of the male's bib is irregular and tends to "feather" into the grayish breast. The female's bib is squared off at the bottom. Despite all these distinguishing marks, one of my friends proposes the following toast to these little beady-eyed friends:

> Here's to the chickadee,
> the sexes are alike you see.
> It's hard to tell the he from she,
> but she can tell, and so can he!

These seemingly carefree birds, which range from central Alaska and Newfoundland south into North Carolina, Indiana, and northwest California, sing two well-loved melodies. Its "chick-a-dee-dee-dee-dee" call ranks first, followed by its high, piercing ''WHEE-dee-dee'' song. On hearing this latter song, scores of people confuse it with that of a phoebe. We've heard this chickadee whistle in every month of the year, more so in spring and early summer.

Students from the University of Wisconsin (Milwaukee), tape recording bird calls at the Cedarburg Bog Field Station, were able to associate about 30 different combinations of chickadee calls, songs, and notes with an equal number of actions, feelings, and mannerisms. Quite a vocabulary!

The fact that so much of its winter food consists of the eggs of harmful insects makes the chickadee a favorite friend of farmers and orchardists.

Of all the chickadees that have trustingly eaten sunflower seeds from our hands, as many or more could not be persuaded to trust us. Some will impatiently fly to one of the empty Koenig feeders and rap sharply against the aluminum siding, over and over, while others gladly take seeds directly from us. I like to think that the obstinate ones are saying, ''OK buddy, hurry up with those seeds. Don't think for one moment that we'd take a chance sitting on your hand!''

Chickadee, rest assured that we trust and respect you as one of our dearest friends.

Snowbirds

My task this day had me down on all ''fours,'' nose within a foot of the bedrock taking photographs of fossils and glacial scratches. An unseasonally warm and pleasant wind was blowing—now gusty, now calm. At the moment, I was arranging my camera equipment for a close-up of what I considered an extraordinary find—a siphuncle of a cephalopod, *Huronia bigsbyi* to be exact. Suddenly I became aware of a series of short, bold, musical warbles. There were birds nearby, and they had been calling all along. But I was so intent upon the fossils that the calls had not quite registered.

When I lifted my head and looked around, I was pleasantly surprised to find that I was virtually surrounded by snow buntings. What a pure sound of joy they produced as they chattered among themselves and scurried about, with nothing but bare rock, muddy little puddles, and the numerous weed stalks that remained from summer's plants. This was too much to resist. I cautiously stood up, hoping to take a picture of them, but was met with a series of sharp whistling calls as they wheeled off—but only a few yards away.

Then began a game of stalking. Did you every stalk snow buntings? Surprising how their flashy black, white, and tan plumage blended with the bedrock and stones. In a moment, they were totally camouflaged by their surroundings. But eventually, their movements gave them away. Although a few splashed in the puddles or picked at gravel, most of them were feeding. Over and over they would flutter up to the higher weed stalks, ride them down to the ground by the force of their weight, then feast upon the seeds that were dislodged—pigweed, ragweed, and spotted knapweed in this case. Always they stayed in a close group. The next time the flock flew up, I thought I noticed two strangers in their midst. My first guess was Lapland longspurs. When I was able to edge in close enough, I confirmed this guess.

As a boy I never heard the snow bunting referred to by any name other than ''snowbird.'' One morning during my first year as an undergraduate in college, I unexpectedly intercepted a large flock of the birds while on the way to school. Being all taken up with the new and challenging venture of learning to be a teacher, I felt an urgent need to identify this flashy black and white beauty. A new world was opening up for me, and I realized that I would be wanting to help young people learn about this snow bunting, too. I believe it was this bird that helped to "open the curtains" for me. Thereafter, every plant and animal I encountered presented a challenge for proper identification.

I experienced another unusual meeting with a snow bunting during my first winter of teaching. A small group of students had become quite interested in collecting and identifying bird nests that had been occupied the previous summer. One boy arrived at school on a Monday morning all excited, and before he opened the box he was carrying, he told us this story.

He and his dad had been hiking along a frozen river looking for nests. They found several without difficulty. One nest was in a cedar tree, about 10 feet off the ground. When he climbed up to retrieve it, he cautiously reached his hand up and into the nest. "I nearly fell out of the tree with excitement," he told us. "There was a bird in there!"

He soon realized that the bird was dead, so down came the nest, bird and all. When he opened the box for us, we saw a beautiful snow bunting, its wings neatly folded, just as though it were sleeping. No marks of injury whatsoever showed on the bird. It was truly a remarkable experience that remains a mystery.

The snow bunting appears to defy the icy blasts of winter blizzards. Let it snow and blow and drift, just so long as enough weed stalks show above the snow. That's all this amazingly hardy creature requires. But come the first part of March, this cold-weather friend of ours begins its migratory flight back north to its summer breeding grounds, the tundra. And if you think we are happy to see the snow buntings arrive here for the winter, just imagine the happiness the Eskimos feel when they see them return in late March, for seldom does the bird make a mistake: When it arrives, so does spring!

There I go, rushing the seasons again, when winter hasn't even begun. Snow bunting, we welcome you to our wintry environment and hope that for generations to come, countless seed-laden weed stalks will continue to grace the open snow-swept fields that you feed upon.

Winter Bandit

We approached the Shoto millpond on a sub-zero January morning hoping to locate one of the rarest winter bird visitors to our state, the northern shrike. John Kraupa assured me that house sparrows were common along the brushy banks of the open water and that it was the sparrows that the shrike was after.

True to John's prediction, we soon saw our bird. Then we located another one as we scanned the surrounding treetops with the spotting scope. This was a ''first'' for me, a ''lifer.'' Undoubtedly I would have seen the bird before this, had I known what to look for and where to look.

This unpredictable black-masked winter bandit sweeps down into the United States from its northern breeding grounds in numbers that increase in four-year cycles. It has been determined that when the mice population reaches a peak, so do the northern shrikes. When the number of mice a particular habitat can support reaches its limit, there is a large, natural die-off of mice. Thereafter, many of the shrikes that must be fed either must move elsewhere to find food or they perish. The number of shrikes reported so far this year indicates that this may be a shrike winter.

When stalking the northern shrike, look for a blue-jay-sized bird with a rather heavy-hooked beak, black mask, large white wing patches, dark wings and tail, and a grayish (brownish when mature) body. It is usually seen perching alone, its tail held quite horizontally. Frequently the bird will be so intent upon watching its prey that one can approach within 20 to 30 feet of it before it flies away. This happened to me in my yard last year. In fact, I had to clap my hands to chase it from its perch no more than 10 feet above my head.

This hardy handsome vagabond has been nicknamed the ''butcherbird.'' Unfortunately, many indoor bird-watchers kill the shrikes that harass ''good'' birds at their feeders. They accuse the shrike of deliberate cruelty, probably basing their conclusions on the bird's feeding habits. For once the shrike has killed its prey, it impales it on the thorn of a tree or even upon the sharp spines of a barbed wire fence. Of course, this is not done out of cruelness. The fact is that shrikes have weak feet and toes. Impaling its prey makes it easier for the shrike to hold its food while eating. It is not uncommon for the bird to store several of its catches for future use.

There is no question in my mind as to the great value of these sleek predatory birds in nature's scheme. Indeed, they help keep other bird populations more stable and, particularly, more healthy. Invariably the strongest of the birds they seek will escape and survive, thereby becoming the healthy breeding stock for the coming spring.

In the early 1900s, the people of Boston learned the value of the shrike. At that time, the English sparrow (now referred to as the house sparrow) was a protected bird. Being slow and plump and somewhat sluggish, it was an easy catch for the shrike! One report has it that shrikes became so abundant on Boston Common that men were hired to shoot them in fear that they would destroy the house sparrows. In one winter alone, one man shot more than 50 shrikes there. It wasn't too long before the Bostonians realized their mistake, however, for soon they had more house sparrows than they had ever hoped for. The tables were abruptly reversed; the shrike became the protected species.

These marvelous birds range well south of Wisconsin during their winter visit, which may extend from October through April. About 60 percent of their diet consists of small birds. The other 40 percent includes insects such as grasshoppers and crickets. However, their preferred food is mice. It has been shown that, during the shrike's summer nesting period in the north, small birds nearby will be left alone as long as there are mice to be captured.

A couple of years ago I encountered a shrike at the Baileys Harbor dump. (Dumps are good places to look for predatory birds because of their attractiveness to starlings and sparrows.) The shrike was perched coyly at the tip of a small aspen tree. I turned the engine of my truck off, rolled the window down, and proceeded to enjoy its company and its waiting game. All the while the shrike absolutely ignored me (or so I thought). Matter of fact, it outwaited me!

As I prepared to leave, I tooted the car horn. This so startled the bird that it tipped backwards suddenly and nearly fell off the branch. But it didn't fly away. I looked into my rearview mirror as I drove off, and there it was, still perched where I had found it and still trying to outsmart its victims. Yes, I'm sure that it succeeded in its quest.

Consider what the shrikes can do for you. Learn the haunts and habits of this magnificent wild brother. Seek them out, and learn from them. Condition your minds and souls to the great and exciting challenges that your own immediate environment offers. Makes life interesting. Try it!

Index

Out on a Limb: A Journal of Wisconsin Birding was designed by Barbara B. Petchenik and edited by David L. Murray. The text is set in 11-point Garamond by WPI of Trenton, New Jersey; the book was printed in a first edition of 3,000 copies by Braun-Brumfield, Inc., Ann Arbor, Michigan. The paper used is 60-pound Warrens 66 Neutral.

PINE STREET PRESS, BAILEYS HARBOR, WISCONSIN—B. & K. PETCHENIK, PROPS.